Abstract

of

Probate Records

Washington County, Ohio

Wills • Estates • Guardianships

1789-1855

Compiled by

BERNICE GRAHAM & ELIZABETH S. COTTLE

CLEARFIELD COMPANY

PREFACE

These Probate Abstracts contain wills, estates
and the guardian records of minors from 1789 to 1855
as contained in the first nine volumes of the Probate
Records of Washington County, Ohio which are kept in
the record room of the Probate Court on the third floor
of the Annex to the Court House in Marietta. No estate
packets are now to be found for this period but in a few
cases it is possible that there may be additional facts
in the Journal of the Court of Common Pleas which had the
original jurisdiction over these matters through 1851.
These Journals are in the custody of the Clerk of
Courts on the third floor of the Court House but most
have been relegated to an attic store room. They are
chronological but unindexed so are suggested only as
a last resort.

The last fiduciary appointments were made in the
Court of Common Pleas at the October, 1851 session and
are recorded in Volume 11 of its Journal. Volume 12
which begins April 5, 1852 has no such appointments
although related cases are still heard on the validity
of a will, assignment of dower and partition of lands.

Ohio's Constitution of 1851 established a separate
Probate Court and new procedures. Thus the first series
of Probate Court Journals begins with Volume A on
February 17, 1852 and continues through Z in 1901. These
also have been placed in an attic storeroom. The most
useful records such as wills probated in 1852 and part
of 1853 have been copied in Probate Record Volume 9
and also petitions up to 1855, abstracts of which are
included here.

With the new Court a new series began, called the
Administrators and Executors Docket. The earliest
volume now on the shelves, Docket B, begins February 17,
1852, the same date as Probate Journal A and is herein
referred to only for cases included in Probate Record
Volume 9.

Separate volumes for wills begin July 13, 1853 with
Volume 1 and again are referred to only for cases recorded in Probate Record Volume 9. Thus the references
here are believed complete through the year 1851 and
for all cases in the first nine volumes of Probate
Records. Further research in the new Dockets and Will
Books will be necessary to complete the years 1852 to
1855 which is a transition period for probate matters.
If the deceased did not leave a will and there was no
petition to sell land to pay debts you will find the
estate listed only in the Administrators and Executors
Docket which also includes all appointments and records
for guardians of minors at this time.

In the earliest years of Washington County,
Ohio included a large area now in other Counties.
Thus there are 25 wills or estates between 1793-1802
for Gallipolis now in Gallia County, several for Middle-
town now in Athens County and one each for Deerfield
now Morgan County and Newton now Muskingum County.
Also there are a few "foreign" wills brought in from
other Ohio Counties and other states.

These nine large volumes of probate records were
read by Bernice Graham or by myself except for the
first 77 pages read by Anita Short, who started a State-
wide Index project. Our County Index was made from the
three sets of notes and checked against the Court House
Index A, the B Docket and Wills Volume 1.

pr 1-9 means Probate Record Vol 1, page 9
B-87b means Administrators and Executors Docket B,
      page 87 and b designates the second of two
      pages with the same number.

The basic facts of names and dates were contributed
to Ohio Wills and Estates to 1850; an Index published in
1981 by Carol Willsey Bell, C.G., completing the work
begun by Anita Short.

Our notes had much more information than that used
in this State Index which we are now sharing with those
doing research in our county. Here you will find the
residence of the deceased, the administrator or the
executor and the heirs when given, sometimes other facts,
all of which we hope you will find useful.

                              Elizabeth S. Cottle

                              Bernice Graham

THE WASHINGTON COUNTY HISTORICAL SOCIETY
acknowledges, with grateful appreciation,
the generous gift of the rights and title
of this book - donated by the co-authors
and compilers - BERNICE GRAHAM and ELIZA-
BETH S. COTTLE, members of The Washington
County Historical Society.

ABBREVIATIONS

admr	administrator
admx	administratrix
B	(Volume of Administrators & (Executors Docket, 1852-1857
c	about
E	Estate, intestate estate
exr	executor
execx	executrix
G	Guardianship record
gdn	guardian
hab.corp	writ of habeas corpus
p	page
P	Petition
pr	Probate Record
Twp	Township
W	Will
wb	Will book, will record

WILLS, ESTATES, GUARDIANSHIPS   (1789-1855)

ABBEY, Elijah   E-1835   pr 5-p 254, 498
                                                   Waterford Twp.
    widow, 5 small children--none named
    Admr - William Bacon

ABBIT, Aaron   E-1800   pr 1-p 37,39
                                                   Marietta

ABORN, Lowry   W-1853   pr 9-p 357, B-72
    of Providence, Providence County,
    R. I. where will probated 1830
    Exrs-wife, Sarah & son, Charles Bowler Aborn

ACKMAN, Eliab B.   E-1834   pr 5-p 147, 563
                                                   Newport Twp.
    widow, 2 children
    Admr-Thomas Ferguson

*ADAMS, Edward   G-1828   pr 4-p 153
    Guardian, John Cotton

ADAMS, Francis   E-1841   pr 6-167
                                                   Marietta Twp.
    Admr - Frederick A. Wheeler

ADAMS, James   E-1823   pr 2-p 451, 453, 455
                                                   Warren Twp.
    Admx - Lucy Adams; Admr - Isaac Humphreys

ADAMS, Joel   E-1820   pr 2-p 196, 197, 215
                                                   pr 3-p 556
                                                   Roxbury Twp.
    widow - Vicey (Lovisay) Adams
    Admr - Dennis Adams

ADAMS, John   E-1827   pr 4-p 29
                                                   pr 7-p 57
                                                   Warren Twp.
    pr 7- p 57 - Final settlement (1844) for
    John Adams and Tiffany Adams, which see.

*ADAMS, Nehemiah C.   G-1828   pr 4-p 154, 379
    Guardian - John Cotton

ADAMS. Tiffany   E-1823   pr 2-p 457, 458
                                                   Warren Twp.
    pr 3-p 97 (4-6-1824, Lucy Dodge called late admx.)
    pr 4-p 30 (property separated from estates of
            John Adams and James Adams)
    pr 7-p 57 (1844) final settlement with that of
            John Adams, which see.
    Admx - Lucy Adams (later Dodge) deceased before settlement
    Admr - Isaac Humphreys

ADDIS, Jonathan   E-1850   pr 8-p 546
                                                         pr 9-p 135
    Admr - Thomas Addis

ADDIS, Thomas   E-1851   pr 9-p 33, 34, 58, 192
                                                         B-24
                                                         Adams Twp.
    children - Jonathan Addis, Jesse Addis, Eliza Ann Gessell,
            Betsey Simons; minor - Rebecca Addis
    Admr - Dan'l Davis

ALCOCK, William   E-1799   pr 1-p 36, 42
                                                         Marietta
    Admx - Sarah Alcock, widow

ALEXANDER, Andrew   W-1815   pr 1-p 280
                                                         Union Twp.
    Wife - Margaretta
    youngest son, John; oldest son, James
    Exrs - Benjamin Franklin Stone of Union
    and son James

ALEXANDER, James   W-1829   pr 4-p 287, 331, 539
                                                         Union
    brother - John
    stepmother - Margaretta Alexander
    Execx - Margaretta Alexander

ALGER, Preserved   W-1821   pr 2-p 214, 232
                                                         Marietta
    wife - Catherine; dau - Cynthia
    Execx - dau Cynthia Crandle

ALLEN, Levi, Jr.   E-1839 (?)   pr 5-p 566
    settlement is in 1839 (but accts. start in 1831)
    Admr - Abijah Brooks

ALLEN, Magdalene   W-1831   pr 4-p 440, 496
        (widow of Reuben Allen)   Belpre
    mentions three sons: Jackson, John & Andrew Allen;
    also Polly Allard, wife of Reuben Allard; Davis
    Allen, son; Betsey Bartlett, wife of William Bartlett;
    grandau Clarisa Allard; Lovisa Blesing.
    Admr - Davis Allen

ALLEN, Reuben   E-1819   pr 2-p178, 179, 400
                                                         pr 3-p199
    widow - Magdelin (Magdalene)   Belpre Twp.
    heirs: Andrew Allen, Mary Allard, Betsy Allen,
           Davis Allen, John Allen, Jackson Allen,
           ? Daniel Goodno ? - signed with heirs
    Admx - Magdaline Allen

ALLISON, Charles   E-1816   pr 1-p 311
                                                         Adams Twp.

```
ALLISON, Hugh                W-1824              pr 3-p155, 201, 204
                                                 pr 4-p 156
      No wife mentioned                          Adams Twp.
      4 sons:  William, Robert, Hugh, Jr., Andrew
      3 daus:  Polly, wife of Frederick Davis; Betsy, wife of
               Morgan Wood; Sally, widow of John Morris, dec'd
      grandch: Eliza, Sally and Betsy Davis, ch of deceased dau, Agnes,
               late wife of Elisha Davis; also, Sally, Polly and Azuba
               Owen, ch of deceased dau Hannah, late wife of Daniel Owen
      Exr - Andrew Allison


ALLISON, Robert              E-1812              pr 1-p 237
                                                 Adams Twp.


AMES, Cyrus                  W-1847              pr 8-p 50, 100
                                                 Belpre Twp.
      sons:  Jesse M., Charles R., William R., & Cyrus, Jr.
      daus - Abigail Brough, wife of Charles H. Brough; Susan Ames,
             Azuba Ames
      daus-in-law:  Mary, wife of Charles R.; Susan, wife of Cyrus, Jr.
      Exr:  son, Cyrus Ames, Jr.


ANDERS, Joseph               W-1852              pr 9-p 187, 218
                                                 B-37
      children                                   Harmar
      Exr - Isaac Spaulding


ANDERSON, Mark               E-1829              pr 4-p 267
                                                 Marietta
      Admr - Otis Wheeler


ANDREWS, Robert              W-1823              pr 2-p 444, 542
                                                 pr 3-p 97, 334
      wife, Electa; brothers, Philander & Jured;    Waterford Twp.
      children of deceased brother, Gideon;
      nephew:  Alanson Deveraux
      Execx - wife Electa Andrews
      Exr - Alanson Devereux (also Devereaux or Deverau)


ANDREWS, Samuel              E-1824              pr 3-p 205
                                                 pr 4-p 68, 208
                                                 pr 5-p 474, 501
      wife, Betsy Andrews                        Waterford Twp.
      children:  all minors, Hannah M., Samuel, Richard,
                 Polly and Hetty Andrews
      Admr - Joseph Morris


APLIN, Oliver                E-1823              pr 5-p 63, 65, 444
                                                 Grandview Twp.
      Admx - Elizabeth Aplin, widow


ARCHER, Benjamin             E-1811              pr 1-p 195, 280
                                                 Wooster Twp.
                                                 (Early name for
      Admr - John T. Deming                      Watertown)
```

ARCHER, Simon   E-1808   pr 1-p 116, 176, 179
  Admx - Nancy Archer   Marietta
  Trustees - Robert Williamson, Obadiah Lincoln, William Hart

ARMSTRONG, Theodosius   E-1842   pr 6-p 338, 339
                     pr 7-p 182
  widow   Belpre Twp.
  Admr - John Ball

ASHCROFT, John   E-1805   pr 1-p 85
  Admrs - Margaret Ashcroft & Samuel Mellor Waterford Twp.

ASHCROFT, (Mrs.) Margaret E-1834   pr 5-p 151, 559
  Admr - Benjamin M. Brown   Watertown

ATCKERSON, Samuel   W-1850   pr 8-p 380, 429, 437, 438
  (also sp. Atcherson, Atkerson, Atkinson) Fearing Twp.
  No wife mentioned
  Children - Hanna, Frederick, Wait, William, Samuel, Ann
      & Elizabeth Atckerson
  Other legatees - Minria Perkins (wife of Asa Perkins); Margaret
         Hall (wife of Joseph Hall); Elizabeth Kelly (wife
         of William Kelly); Benford Croy; William Croy,
         Edith Morris
  Exr - John Collins

ATKINSON, John   E-1818   pr 2-p 107, 191
  Admr - Payton R. Fearing   Wesley Twp.

AYLES, David   W-1850   pr 8-p 401
                     pr 9-p 36, 40, 413, 464
  wife - Susan   Aurelius Twp.
  sons & daus - Betsy Pugh, Elias Ayles, Hannah Low,
       Louisa Kitts, Paton Ayles
  Exrs - wife, Susan Ayles & Joel Tuttle

BABCOCK, Joseph   E-1823   pr 2-p 450, 451
                     pr 3-p 295
  widow & heirs mentioned, not named   Marietta
  Admr - John Crawford

*BABCOCK, Louisa M.   Guardian Accts.
  nee Louise M. Morse, which see.

BACKUS, Matthew   E-1808   pr 1-p 180, 188

BAGLEY, Henry   E-1793   pr 1-p 11, 13
  Admr - Dr. Jabez True   Marietta

*BAHRENBURG, Cord   G-1848   pr 8-p 189
   (insane)
  Guardian - Thomas F. Stanley

BAILEY, John J.   E-1849   pr 8-p 270, 357, 359
                                               pr 9-p 411, 464
    widow - Mary C. Bailey   Warren Twp.
    minor ch - Sarah & John W.
    Admr - William P. Cutler

BAKER, John C.   E-1838   pr 5-p 514
                                               Marietta

BAKER, Samuel   W-1805   pr 1-p 88, 89, 306 (1816)
                                               pr 2-p 73
    wife - Roda   Waterford
    sons - Seth, Samuel
    daus - Roda, Sally
    Exrs - named in will - William Gray & wife, Roda
    Admr de bonis non - Titan Kimble (1816)

BAKER, Samuel, Jr.   E-1816   pr 1-p 306
    Admr - Titan Kimble, also admr of father's estate

BALDWIN, Jonathan   E-1816   pr 1-p 298, 299, 300
                                               pr 2-p 22, 87, 126
    Admr - Thomas White   Roxbury Twp.

BALL, Cadwalader C.   E-1843   pr 7-p 18
    Admr - William A. Whittlesey

BALL, George   E-1827   pr 4-p 64, 108
                                               Decatur Twp.

BALLOU, Arnold   E-1841   pr 6-p 215
                                               Marietta
    Admx - Mary Ballou

BARBER, Levi   W-1833   pr 5-p 2, 293
                                               Marietta
    wife - unnamed
    children - David, Elizabeth, Austin, Levi
    friend - John P Mayberry
    Exr - David Barber (son)

*BARKER, Isaac   G-1802   pr 1-p 48, 50
                                               Middletown Twp.
    charged with non-support of family by overseers   (now Athens County)
    of Poor of Middletown Twp. Guardians apptd
    for him (not his children)

BARKER, Joseph   E-1844   pr 7-p 100, 113
                                               pr 8-p 246
    Admr - Joseph Barker, Jr. (of Lower Newport)   Union Twp.

BARNS, Samuel   E-1800   pr 1-p 37, 46, 257
                                               Middletown Twp. (later
    (also Barnes)   Athens Co.) and
    Admr - Isaac Peirce   Belpre Twp.

BARRETT, John   E-1825   pr 3-p 456, 559
     heir is sister, Bridget Phair, residence unknown   Marietta

     First admr - not given
     Admr de bonis non - Caleb Emerson

BARSTOW, Caleb   E-1823   pr 3-p 1
                                         Marietta

BARSTOW, Isaac   E-1826   pr 3-p 517, 519
     widow - Frances Barstow   pr 4-p 95, 369
     children - Adaline, of age; minors - Cynthia,   Newport Twp.
           Horace, Henry & Achsey (Achsah)
     Admr - Joseph Barker, Jr.

BARTLETT, Jeremiah   E-1813   pr 1-p 256
                                         pr 2-p 231
     Admx - Jerusha Bartlett   Union Twp.

*BARTLETT, Jeremiah   G-1854   pr 9-p 572
                                         B-224 to 226
     Eliza, Henry & William   Union Twp.

     Guardian and father, Levi Bartlett, states that these are
     minor children of Maria Bartlett dec'd and heirs of
     real estate of Solomon Dickey, their grandfather

BARTLETT, Joseph   E-1823   pr 3-p 14, 17, 336
     Admrs - Sarah Bartlett & William Bartlett   Marietta

BARTMESS, Henry   E-1824   pr 3-p 176, 177
                                         pr 4-p
     widow - Martha   Fearing Twp.
     Admr - Jacob Bartmess

BASIM, Henry   E-1852   pr 9,p 333, 336, 395
     widow - Nancy (died before 4-21-1853)   B-59
     Admr - Joseph Basim   Decatur Twp.

BASIM, Jacob   E-1852   pr 9-p 330, 332, 356
     (also spelled BASOM)   B-56, 159-161, 168, 279, 28
     widow - Avah (Ivy)   Fairfield Twp.
     minor children - Elizabeth, Henry, Eliza
     Admr - Shelton Dunbar

BATCHELDER, Freeman   E-1846   pr 7-p 431, 434, 457
                                         Decatur Twp.
     widow and children mentioned but not named
     Admr - Philip Shrader, Jr.

BEACH, Asa   E-1846   pr 7-p 329, 339, 343
                                         pr 8-p 469
     widow - Elizabeth   Watertown Twp.
     Admrs - Jesse Beach & David Beach

BEACH, Jesse   E-1798   pr 1-p 32
     Admr - Asa Beach   Waterford Twp.

*BEEBE, Mary & William   G-1833   pr 5-p 50
    Children of Dr. William Beebe, their guardian's
    petition to sell land
    Guardian - Oliver R. Loring

BEEBE, Dr. William   E-1821   pr 2-p 235, 236
                                                  pr 4-p 166
    widow - Mary Beebe, later m--Blizzard   pr 5-p 50
    children - Mary & William Beebe, minors   Belpre Twp.
    with guardian, Oliver R. Loring
    pr 5-p 50, petition for his children's gdn. to sell land
    Admrs - Charles Beebe, O. R. Loring

BELL, Frederick   W-1834   pr 5-p 143, 208, 227, 276, 304
                                                  Barlow Twp.
    wife - Hannah
    oldest son, Nathan; son William
    daus - Elizabeth, Margaret, Sophia, Jane & Maryan
    Exr - Nathan Bell (son)

BELL, James   W-1853   pr 9-p 357, 387, 464
                                                  B-71
    wife - Margaret   Salem Twp.
    son - James
    daus - Marion Simonds (husband, Edmund), Margaret Jackson,
           Alison Carlin, Betsy Hall, Katharine Bell
    Exr - Ely Vaughan (friend)

BELL, Samuel   E-1844   pr 7-p 134, 137
                                                  pr 8-p 38, 97
    Admr - Joseph Bell   Marietta Twp.

BELLOWS, William C.   E-1841   pr 6-p 245, 393
                                                  Belpre Twp.
    Admr - David White

BENEDICT, Levi   W-1824   pr 3-p 156, 207, 208, 547
                                                  pr 6-p 89
    wife - Charlotte
    legatee - nephew, George Benedict under guardianship
             of Ebenezer Benedict
    Exr - George Dana

BENT, Daniel   W-1828   pr 4-p 130, 184, 187
                                                  Belpre
    wife - Elizabeth (Betsey), dau Jane
    natural son - Lewis Bent (mother, Polly Misner)
    natural dau - Lucy Bent or Lucy Leach (mother, Deborah Leach)
    remainder to Mrs. Susan Oaks, Nahum Bent, Abner Bent & Dorcas
    Dana (relation not given)
    Admx - Betsey Bent, widow

BENT, Mary   E-1831   pr 4-p 562
                                                  pr 5-p 124
    Admr - Nahum Bent

BENT, Silas   E-1818   pr 2-p 99, 101, 102, 180
                                                         Pr 4-p 161
     widow - Mary   Belpre Twp.
     heirs named at settlement: George Smith for Polly B.
     Smith, Susanna Oakes, William Dana for Dorcas, his wife;
     Daniel Bent & Silas Bent, Jr.
     Admr - Daniel Bent

BERKINSHA, John   E-1839   pr 6-p 44, 320
                                                         Belpre Twp.
     (also Birkensha)
     widow - Hannah
     named, also, John Berkinsha & Polly Berkinsha
     Admr - Bial Stedman

BERKINSHA, Polly   W-1850   pr 8-p 404
                                                         Belpre
     Legatees - Daniel Goss, Lydia Goss, Sarah Maria Hibbard,
                Diantha Jane Rosecrans, Lucy Dorcas Rosecrans;
                also, sisters, Lucretia Root, Sally, Polly
                and Sarah M. Hibbard
     Exr - not named in Will

BERRY, Elizabeth   E-1846   pr 7-p 341, 343
                                                         pr 8-p 149
     Admr - David Hays   Jolly Twp.

BERRY, Jacob   E-1790   pr 1-p 4
     Soldier in service of U.S.
     Admr - James Cox (recommended by Capt. Ziegler)

BERTHÉ, Lewis   E-1796   pr 1-p 21, 25
                                                         Gallipolis
     Admr - Hannah Mion Berthé, widow

BIGGINS, Thomas   E-1850   pr 8-p 524, 529, 531
                                                         pr 9-p 116
     Admr - Daniel N. Dunsmoor   Barlow Twp.

BINEGAR, Jonathan   W-1850   pr 8-p 512
     John W. Binegar
     dau - Margaret Ann Flemming
     No exr named in will

BIRD, Clarence   W-1830   pr 4-p 320
     of Troy, Rensselaer Co., N.Y.
     where will was probated in 1828

     legatees - David Buel, Jr. of Troy
                William A. Bird of Black Roll;
                also, Augustus Buel, grandson of David Buel
     Exrs - David Buel, Jr. and William A. Bird

BIRD, John   W-June, 1846   pr 7-p 357

    of Troy, Rensselaer Co., N.Y.
    where will was proved first, but no date
    (will written 1805, codicil 1806)
    proved May, 1846 in Hocking Co., Ohio

    wife; two sons, John Hampden Bird of Burlington, Vt.,
        and Clarence Bird
    Exrs - (friends) - Col. Albert Pawling, Ebenezer Wilson &
                Benjamin Smith

BIRD, Dr. Seth   W-1846   pr 7-p 354

    of Litchfield, Conn.
    where will proved in 1805

    dau - Minerva, wife of James Stoddard
    dau - Sarah Bird
    son - John Bird of Troy, Rensselaer Co., N.Y.

    Exr - son, John Bird

*BISHOP, Nancy   G-1819   pr 2-p 146

    neé Dexter
    former wife of Abraham Bishop
    now single and a lunatic
    Petition to sell Ohio lands which she inherited
    from father, Timothy Dexter and brother Samuel Lord
    Dexter) both of Newburyport, Mass.) to pay debts with
    Power of Atty. granted to Benjamin P. Putnam to do this.
    Guardian - Gilbert Frothingham of Newburyport, Essex Co., Mass.

BLAKE, Benjamin   E-1823   pr 3-p 10
                                               pr 4-p 11,85
    widow - Lucy Blake   Fearing Twp.
    other heirs mentioned but not named
    Admrs - Thomas F. Stanley & Lucy Blake

BLANCET, David   E-1823   pr 3-p 8, 297
                                               Fearing Twp.
    Admr - Thomas F. Stanley
    (above name also spelled Blansett)

BLANCHARD, Augustus   E-1830   pr 4-p 513
    of Milford, Hillsborough Co., N.H.
    where estate was probated earlier but no date given

    widow - Bridget Blanchard now of Leominster, Mass.
    9 children who survive and
    heirs of a deceased daughter
    Admr - Solomon K. Livermore of Milford, N.H.

BLISS, Amos   E-1792   pr 1-p 10, 12, 146, 147
                                                         Marietta

    wife - Phebe
    children - Polly, Sally & Lydia Bliss
    Admx - Phebe Bliss who mar. Moses Elwell and
           lived Brattleborough, Windham Co., Vt.

BLIZZARD, Brooks   E-1851   pr 8-p618
                                                         pr 9-p 5, 57, 360
    widow   Marietta Twp.
    Admr - William Beebe

BODWELL, Elijah   E-1793   pr 1-p 11
                                                         Gallipolis
    Admr - John Mathews of Gallipolis,
           a partner in trade with dec'd

BOIES, William   E-1823   pr 2-p 514, 517
                                                         pr 3-p 189
    Admr - George Bowen   Waterford

BOSTON, Michael   W-1845   pr 7-p 142, 206
                                                         pr 8-p 281
    wife - Rachael   Liberty Twp.
    sons - John, Michael, George G., Jacob, Thomas,
           William, Leander
    daus - Katharine, Mary, Lovina and Rachel Elinor
    Exr - Jacob Thomas (friend)

BOSWORTH, Charles   E-1841   pr 6-p 260, 467
    widow   Marietta Twp.
    4 children under age 15   (Town of Harmar)
    Admrs - D. P. Bosworth & D. Putnam, Jr.

*BOSWORTH, Henry Martin   G-1853   pr 9-p 500
    Daniel P., Jr., Frank H &   B-155
    George Wells, minors

    Guardian - Daniel P. Bosworth says his wards are children
    of Deborah T. Wells Bosworth, dec'd, and share in estate
    of grandparents - Martyn and Deborah F. Wells with lands
    in Maine which he petitions to sell.

BOSWORTH, Joseph   W-1830   pr 4-p 322, 364, 516, 564
                                                         Marietta
    dau - Mary Babcock, once Mary Bosworth
    grandson - George Claghorn Babcock
    granddau - Sarah Bosworth Fearing once Sarah Bosworth Babcock
    Exr - George C. Babcock

```
BOSWORTH, Sala                W-1823              pr 2-p 440
                                                  pr 3-p 211
    wife - mentioned but not named                pr 4-p 4
    son - Zephaniah and his wife Lucy             Marietta
    sons - Daniel, Charles, Sala, Jr., and John William
    daus - Amanda, Clarissa, Deborah & Selina

    Exrs - Charles & Denial P. Bosworth


BOSWORTH, Zadock              E-1841              pr 6-p 145, 256
                                                  pr 8-p 232
    Admr - William A. Bosworth                    Newport Twp.

BOWEN, William                W-1835              pr 5-p 250
                                                  pr 7-p 104
    of Providence, R. I. where
    will probated 1832

    daus - Elizabeth Amory, Sarah Skinner, Harriet Morris,
          Maria Whipple, wife of John Whipple
    grandson - William C. Bowen

    Exrs - son-in-law, John Whipple of Providence &
          Charles Morris of Charleston, Suffolk Co., Mass.

BOWERS, Henry                 W-1845              pr 7-p 245
    of New York City
    where will probated 1800

    wife - Mary
    son - John M.
    daus - Rebecca & Harriet

    Execx - Wife - Mary: (father-in-law, John R. Meyers & son-in-law
            James C. Duane, named in will but not appt by Court.)

BOWERS, Janna R.              E-1823              pr 2-p 397
                                                  pr 4-p 26
    (also sp Jana, Jena & Jener)                  Marietta
    Admr - Darius Hartshorn

BOWHAN, Martin T.             E-1852              pr 9-p 321, 361, 362
                                                  B- 57
    Admr - Jacob Bowhan                           Salem Twp.

BRADEL - see - PRADEL

BRADFORD, Robert              W-1823              pr 2-p 387, 404
    wife - Lois                                   Belpre
    daus - Sally Pier & Sophia (minor)
    sons - Samuel Adams Bradford, Robert, Jr., &
          Otis L. Bradford
    Exr - Otis L. Bradford
```

BREAKENRIDGE, David   E-1843   pr 7-p 33, 35, 115, 194
                                                     Barlow Twp.
      p. 194 mentions dec'd bro Andrew & heirs, Neil,
            David, Margaret, Duncan & Charles McV.
            Breakenridge
      Admr - Thomas Breakenridge

BREAKENRIDGE, David   E-1849   pr 8-p 369, 371, 381
                                                     pr 9-p 65
      widow - Margaret   B-176
      minor children - Jeannet & Mary Ann   Barlow Twp.
      Admr - George Breakenridge

BREAKENRIDGE, Hugh   E-1838   pr 5-p 541, 543
                                                     pr 6-p 70
      widow & heirs, not named   Watertown Twp.
      Admr - John Breakenridge

BRECK, John   E-1816   pr 1-p 307
                                                     pr 2-p 65, 98, 137, 216
      widow - Anna   pr 4-p 80
      unnamed children   Salem Twp.
      Admrs - Daniel G. Stanley & Anna Breck
            who later mar._____ Salmon

*BRECK, William F.   G-1840   pr 6-p 90

      Guardian - George Dana

BRIDGES, Benjamin   W-1841   pr 6-p 187, 225, 466
                                                     Belpre Twp.
      sons - Morris Bridges & Jacob Bridges
      daus - Minerva Haight; Rebecca Withington, wife of
            Francis Withington; & Eliza Bridges, who
            mar. _____Haight before settlement (1843)
      Exr - Jacob Bridges (son)

BRIGGS, John   E-1802   pr 1-p 48, 52
                                                     Newtown Twp.
      Admr - John Briggs   (now Muskingum County)

BRIGGS, Zadock   W-1823   pr 2-p 430
                                                     pr 3-p 1, 4
      wife - Sally   Adams Twp.
      sons - Henri, Ansel, Zara, Marcus, Franklin
      son-in-law - Eli Fox
      daus - Asenath Jacobs, Sally Hayns & Polly Vercy
      Exr - Ansel Briggs

BRIGHAM, Elizabeth   E-1841   pr 6-p 270, 277, 443
                                                     Marietta Twp.
      Admr - Lucius Brigham

BRITTON, James   W-1833   pr 5-p 3, 67, 69, 262
                                                     Fearing Twp.
      wife - Sarah
      sons - Nathan, James, Levi & John
      dau - Jane; other children
      Exrs - John Collins & Walter Athey

```
BROOKS, Samuel              E-1823              pr 2-p 406, 407, 511
                                               Union Twp.
   widow and children, unnamed
   Admr - Abijah Brooks

*BROOKS, Samuel H.          G-1853              pr 9-p 470
       John A., minors                         B-109, 113, 338

   Guardian - John Dodge petition to sell land in
              Beverly together with William M. Brooks

BROOMBACK, Martin          E-1853              pr 9-p 454, 456, 461, 566
                                               B-70, 165
   widow - Catharine                           Warren Twp.
   Admr - William D. Bailey

BROUGH, Bridget            W-1822              pr 2-p 255, 272, 278
                                               pr 3-p 302
   late Bridget Cross                          Marietta
   pr 3-p 302- settlement (1825) of her estate with
              that of former husband, Waid Cross
   present husband - John Brough who died c. May, 1823
   dau - Mary Baker, wife of John Baker of Dutchess Co., N.Y.
   Exr - John Brough
   Admr de bonis non-1  Davidson Murray
   Admr de bonis non-2  Caleb Emerson

BROUGH, John               E-1823              pr 2-p 310, 313
                                               pr 3-p 118, 290
   2 wives preceded him in death               pr 4-p 282, 386, 436
   5 children - Jane who marr. Hugh Ferry; Mary Ann; Marietta
               John (Jr.); Charles H.; & William P.
               Brough

*BROUGH, John (Jr.)        G-1830              pr 4-p 436
        Charles H.
        William P.
   children of John Brough, Sr. - dec'd 1823
   petition to sell land

   Guardian - Ebenezer Gates

*BROUGH, Mary Ann          G-1830              pr 4-p 386
   dau of John Brough, Sr., dec'd 1823
   Petition to sell land as she owns an undivided
   fifth part of farm with sister, Jane and three brothers

   Guardian - Hugh Ferry (mar. to her sister, Jane)

BROWN, James               W-1837              pr 5-p 380
   of Providence, R. I.
   where will presented, 1834
   heirs omitted - (see original)

   Exr - nephew, John Brown Francis of Warwick, R. I.
```

```
BROWN, Jesse                    E-1816              pr 1-p 309
                                                    pr 2-p 57, 86
     Admr - Theophilus H. Powers                    Waterford Twp.

BROWN, John                     E-1816              pr 1-p 302
                                                    pr 3-p 263, 296
     widow & heirs mentioned but not named          Waterford Twp.
     Admr - Amasa Davis

BROWN, John                     E-1839              pr 6-p 1, 51, 349
     widow & 2 children (under 14) not named        Harmar
     Admr - John Crawford

BROWN, Nicholas                 W-1842              pr 6-p 382
     of Providence, R. I.
     where will probated in 1841
     heirs omitted

     Exrs - son, John Carter Brown & nephews,
            Moses B. & Robert H. Ives

BROWNING, Isaac                 E-1809              pr 1-p 174
                                                    Fearing Twp.

BROWNING, William               E-1823              pr 2-p 519, 524
                                                    pr 3-p 209
     Admr - William R. Browning                     pr 5-p 449 (1837)
                                                    Belpre Twp.

BROWNING, William R.            W-1851              pr 9-p 18, 21, 80, 324
     wife - Sophia                                  B-17
     dau - Sophia                                   Belpre Twp.
     grandson - William B. Knapp
     sons - William, Alexander Hamilton &
            deceased Joseph W.
     nephew - Arthur Browning
     cousin - James Smith of Philadelphia
     Admrs - Alexander H. Browning & Benjamin F. Stone

BRUCE, Almer                    E-1852              pr 9-p 151, 370
     widow - Laurena W.                             B-4
     minor children under 15 - Robert,             Marietta Twp.
          Napoleon B., Wallace, Friend, Bernard D.
     Admr - Thomas Maxwell

BRUMPTON, Robert                W-1836              pr 5-p 290
     Sergeant in Capt. Haskell's Company, U.S. Army

     friend - James Patterson
     Admr - John D. Chamberlain
```

```
BRUNIER, Firmin              E-1796              pr 1-p 20
    Admr - Stephen Chandivert                    Gallipolis


BRYAN, John                  E-1790              pr 1-p 5
    U. S. Soldier
    Admr - John Chambers


BUCKLEY, Thomas              W-1847              pr 7-p 468
    of New York City
    where will probated (proved) 1846
    wife - Anna
    sons - John L. Buckley & Phineas H. Buckley
    grandchildren - Edward M. & Ann M. (children of deceased son,
                            Effingham L. Buckley)
    daus - Mary Ann Wood & Jane L. Buckley
    Exrs - John L. Buckley & Phineas H. Buckley


BUCKMAN, Jacob               E-1801              pr 1-p 45, 50
    also sp. Burkman                             Marietta

    Admr - Joseph Buell


BUELL, Daniel H.             W-1843              pr 7-p 13, 43, 45, 138, 266
    wife - Theodocia                             Marietta
    3 minor children - Henry Joseph Buell, Edward Wyllys
                        Buell, William H. Buell
    Exr - William Slocomb


BUELL, Ebenezer              E-1802              pr 1-p 50
    Admrs - Joseph Buell & Timothy Buell         Marietta


BUELL, Joseph                E-1812              pr 1-p 213, 222, 224,
                                                        230, 231
    widow                                        Marietta
    children - Frances Buell, Daniel Hand Buell,
               William Henry Buell, Hiram Augustus Buell,
               Mary Ann Buell, Silva Buell, Joseph Buell
    Admrs - Timothy Buell & Daniel H. Buell


BUELL, Salmon D.             E-1823              pr 3-p 11, 13, 420
                                                 pr 4-p 249
    widow - Eliza Buell                          Adams Twp.
    children - (unnamed) have Timothy Buell
               as Guardian
    Admr - P. B. Buell


BUELL, Timothy               W-1837              pr 5-p 358, 398, 401,
                                                        467, 575
    3rd wife - Laurana, survived him             pr 6-p 28, 194
    children - 2 of whom were minors, one of these   Marietta Twp.
               being William P. Buell
    Exr - Ebenezer D. Buell (son)
```

```
BUELL, William H.                E-1821            pr 2-p 227, 228, 263
    widow - Lavina Buell                            pr 3-p 318, 426
    infant heir - Frances Ann Buell                 pr 4-p 542
    Admr - Weston Thomas                            pr 6-p 90
                                                    Marietta


BULKLEY, Roger                   W-1852            pr 9-p 268
    of          , County of                         B-57
New London, Conn.
where probated 1819
wife - Mary
sons - Benjamin R., Gershom. Roger
grandchildren - Eliza L., John A., Augustus W.,
                Caroline & Aurelia Bulkley
Exrs - Benjamin R. Bulkley, Daniel Watrous


*BULLARD, Franke C.               G-1852            pr 9-p 181
    and Henrie T.                                   B-30
of Indianapolis, Indiana
heirs of Susan P. Bullard, dec'd

    Guardian - Talbut Bullard petitions to sell Marietta land
               Susan P. Bullard received of Dr. John Cotton


BUNDY, Benjamin                  W-1853            pr 9-p 376, 388, 389, 462
                                                    B- 75
    wife - Rachel                                   Wesley Twp.
    children - not named except minors - Ester &
               Lindly who got yr's support
    Exrs - Rachel Bundy & Thomas Bundy, Jr.


BUNDY, David                     E- 1844           pr 7-p 77, 90
                                                    pr 8-p 236
    widow - Achsah Bundy                            Wesley Twp.
    minor son - Joel Bundy
    Admr - William Bundy


BUNDY, Eli                       E-1839            pr 6-p 57
                                                    pr 8-p 558
    widow - Sarah                                   Roxbury Twp.
    unnamed children
    Admrs - William Smith & Ezekiel Bundy


*BUNDY, Joel                      G-1852            pr 9-p 122
    Guardian - Thomas Bundy


BURCH, Ephraim                   E-1825            pr 3-p 281, 359
                                                    pr 4-p 90, 228
    widow - not named                               Adams Twp.
    minor children - Mehaly, Mary, John and
                     Thursey Burch
    Admr - Andrew Allison
```

*BURCHARD, Caroline L.   G-1854   pr 9-p 570
                                                B-184
     Guardian - George M. Woodbridge
     Petition to sell land as owner of warrant for 160 acres
     of land issued 6-14-1853 to Reuben W. Northrup and Henry
     A. Northrup, children of and to Caroline L. Burchard,
     grandchildren of Thurston Northrup, a private in Third
     Reg. + U. S. Rifleman

BURLINGAME, Susanna   W-1840   pr 6-p 116
     dau. of Gen. Rufus Putnam   Marietta
     husband - Christopher Burlingame
     son - John B. Burlingame
     other sons & daus

     Exrs - Edwin & John B. Burlingame

BURLINGAME, Christopher   W-1841   pr 6-p 249, 274
     to friend, Douglas Putnam in trust for   pr 8-p 190
     dau Charlotte H. Burlingame, wife of John Burlingame
     Exr - Douglas Putnam

BURNSIDE, Patrick   E-1821   pr 2-p 219, 220
                                               pr 3-p 413
     widow - Nancy Burnside   Decatur Twp.
     heirs of full age - William Burnside; Charlotte
     DeBolt & William DeBolt, her husband; Susanna
     Burnside & Ephraim Burnside; also minor children
     of John Burnside, dec'd. (viz: Susanne & Betsy
     Burnside); also, heirs outside of jurisdiction
     of this court: Benjamin & Samuel Burnside

     Admr - Asa Morey

BURRIS, John   W-1850   pr 8-p 548
                                               Grandview Twp.
     present wife - Eleanor
     youngest dau - minor, Lovina Burris, present wife's child
     sons - Martin, John
     Lovina Burris - first wife's child
     children of son, David - Martin William Burris &
                              Nancy Elizabeth
     other children - Benjamin Burris, Van Burris,
                      Swerenghen Burris & Stincin Burris

     Exr - William Rea, also to be guardian of Lovina Burris

BURROUGHS, Jacob   E-1834   pr 5-p 197, 199, 313

     Admr - William Burroughs

BURROUGHS, Jarvis   E-1823   pr 4-p 605, 614
                                               pr 5-p 88, 135
     widow - Susan   Belpre
     dau - Amanda (minor)

     Admr - Benjamin F. Stone

                              Washington County, Ohio Probate -17-

BURROUGHS, Thomas   E-1826   pr 3-p 523, 525
                                                    pr 6-p 158
    Admr - Jarvis Burroughs; then
    Admr de bonis non - William Burroughs

BURROWAY, Isaac   E-1802   pr 1-p 51, 53
    Admr - John Mackenwelder

CADOT, Claude   E-1797   pr 1-p 22, 26, 28
    Admx - Jane Cadot, widow   Gallipolis

CADWELL, Alice   W-1848   pr 8-p 101, 125
    (single)   Marietta
    brother - James Cadwell
    sister - Margaret Fearnley
    children of dec'd brother - Peter Cadwell:
            Mary Ann Matthews, John Cadwell, Margaret
            Locherone
    Exrs - bro. James Cadwell & Peter Fearnley

*CADWELL, Alice Jane   G-1851   pr 8-p 567, 568, 569
    Lucy E., John
    ch. of James Cadwell, dec'd
    Guardian - Robert Crawford

CADWELL, James   E-1848   pr 8-p 204, 207, 560
    4 minor children - Sarah, John Thomas, Alice Jane
            & Lucy Eliza, last three under
            age 15

    Admr - Weston Thomas

CADWELL, John   W-1837   pr 5-p 451, 485, 488
    names brother James Cadwell, sister Alice   pr 6-p 4, 32
    Cadwell, sister Margarette Fearnley, wife of   Marietta
    Peter Fearnley; 3 children of dec'd bro. Peter Cadwell
    (i.e. Mary Ann, John & Margarette Cadwell)
    Exrs - bro. James Cadwell & Peter Fearnley

CADWELL, Richard   W-1835   pr 5-p 217
    (single)   Marietta

    heirs are bros & sisters: John Cadwell; James
    Cadwell; Alice Cadwell; Margaret Fearnley, wife
    of Peter Fearnley; also, children of bro. Peter
    Cadwell, dec'd: Mary Ann, John & Margaret

    Exrs - bro. John Cadwell & sister Margaret

CALDER, Alexander   W-1849   pr 8-p 249, 262, 263, 272
    wife   pr 9-p 53
    sons - John, Alexander, William, David, Phillip C.; Warren Twp.
            Vanburen & Wallace
    widow of James M. Calder;
    daus - Margaret Swan; Eliza Slater; Phebe Tilton

    Admr - Judson J. Hollister

CALLAHAN, John   E-1843   pr 6-p 478
    also CALIHAN   pr 7-p 59
                                                Waterford Twp.
    Admr - John Callahan, Jr.

CAMOCK, John   E-1816   pr 1-p 310

CAMRON, John   W-1849   pr 8-p 344, 374, 375,
    (also CAMERON)   382, 596
                                                Grandview Twp.
    wife - Esther
    dau - Mariah (single)
    son-in-law - Edward Shapley
    Admr with will annexed - William Little,
                        the widow declining

*CARPENTER, Christopher C.   G-1847   pr 8p- 24

    Guardian Accts. 1841-1847
    Guardian - James Withum

CARTER, Benjamin Bowen   W-1840   pr 6-p 112
    of New York City, where will was probated
    1830, but formerly of Providence, R. I. &
    son of John Carter, dec'd

    3 sisters - Rebecca C. Jencks, Huldah M. Carter
            & Elizabeth A. Danforth, all of
            Providence, R. I.
    property includes share of lands in the
    Ohio Company's purchase
    Execx - Huldah M. Carter (sister)

CARTER, Huldah Maria   W-1850   pr 8-p 444
    single woman of Providence, R. I.
    where will probated in 1842

    sister - Elizabeth Ann Danforth, wife of Walter R.
            Danforth; nephew - Andrew Jackson Danforth;
            niece - Sophia Baines Danforth

    bro - Crawford Carter
    nephews - Francis C. Jenckes & Amos Throop Jenckes,
            children of dec'd sister, Rebecca C. Jenckes

    Exr - John Carter Brown

*CARTER, Margaret Jane   G-1851   pr 8-p 599
    child of John J. Carter, dec'd
    Guardian - Thomas Henton
    rec'd legacy from estate of John Henton (1847)

CARTER, Richard   E-1845   pr 7-p 227, 229, 318, 319
                                                pr 9-p 59
    Admr - John H. Livezy

CARVER, Elizer   E-1823   pr 3-p 18, 20, 145, 438,478
     widow - Mary   Marietta
     family
     Admr - Timothy Buell

CASE, John   E-1802   pr 1-p 51, 53, 77
                                                      Gallipolis
     Admx - Betsey Case
     Admr - Brewster Higby

CASE, Mary   W-1820   pr 2-p 174, 193, 208, 209
     granddau - Eliza Allcock   Marietta
     daus - Polly Cone & Hannah Wells
     sons - William M., Zenas, Shadrick, Timothy..
          & Augustus
     Exr - William M. Case

CASE, Zenas   W-1811   pr 1-p 193
     wife - Mary   Marietta
     sons - Augustus, William M., Zenas, Shadrack
          & Timothy
     daus - Polly Cole, Elizabeth Alcock &
          Hannah Case
     granddau - Polly Case

     Exrs - wife - Mary & Augustus Case - son

CAYWOOD, Joseph   E-1840   pr 6-p 118, 149, 394
     (CAWOOD)   Lawrence Twp.
     widow - Elizabeth Caywood
     Admr - Thomas Cawood

CHAMBERLAIN, Prudence D.   E-1844   pr 7-p 60,111
                                                      pr 8-p 27
     Admr - John D. Chamberlain   B-104

*CHAMBERS, Cornelius R.   G-1843   pr 7-p 22
                                                      pr 8-p 190 (1848)
     (son of William Chambers, Jr., dec'd -
      see W-1838)
     Guardian - John Chambers, his father's bro.

*CHAMBERS, Eleanor   G-1831   pr 4-p 506 - settlement
     (dau of John Chambers, now Eleanor Hoff)

     Guardian - William Nixon

CHAMBERS, Hiram   E-1852   pr 9-p 337
                                                      B-50
     widow - Amanda A.   Marietta
     minor ch - Otis J., Salmon M., Mary S.,
               Sarah C.
     Admx - Amanda Chambers

CHAMBERS, James G.   E-1848   pr 8-p 140, 171, 172
                                                      pr 9-p 346
     Admr - John Crawford, then   B-61, 140
     Admr de bonis non - Thomas W. Ewart   Lawrence Twp.

CHAMBERS, John   W-1823   pr 2-p 422, 473, 476
    wife - Ann   pr 4-p 55, 70
    son - James, of age   Lawrence Twp.
    9 minor children - Thomas, Joseph, Sally Ann,
                       Eleanor, Hezekiah, Hiram and
                       Mary with William Nixon as gdn

                       and Joshua & Greer with Junia
                       Jennings as guardian
    Admrs - William Nixon & James G. Chambers (son)

*CHAMBERS, Mary   G-1831   pr 4-p 506
    (dau of John Chambers)

    settlement includes agreement with James Hoff, 2nd
    who married her sister, Eleanor

    Guardian - William Nixon

*CHAMBERS, Thomas et al   G-1829   pr 4-p 254
    (son of John & Ann Chambers)
    other children are: Joseph, Sally Ann, Eleanor,
                         Joshua, Greer, Hezekiah, Hiram
                         & Mary (also children of John &
                         Ann Chambers)

    Guardian - William Nixon

CHAMBERS, Thomas   W-1852   pr 9-p 174
    wife - Prudence   B-36
    daus - Mary Jane Preston, Caroline M. Smith, Wesley Twp.
           Eleanor B. Chambers

    Exrs - Edwin T. Preston & John S. Smith

CHAMBERS, William   E-1840   pr 6-p 172
                                                  pr 8-p 113
    Admr - John Chambers   Lawrence Twp.

CHAMBERS, William, Jr.   W-1838   pr 5-p 532, 550
                                                  pr 6-p 316
    only son - Cornelius Richard Chambers, for whom Lawrence Twp.
               he appoints his brother, John Chambers
               as guardian

    Exr - John Chambers (brother)

CHAMPLIN, Christopher Grant   W-1840   pr 6-p 102
    of Newport, R. I. and Providence
    Plantations, where will proved, 1840
    then copy sent to Ohio

    wife - Martha Redwood Champlin
    nephews - George Champlin Mason, Jr.
              Benjamin Augustus Mason
              Christopher Grant Perry
    & many other heirs (omitted) but
    no sons or daus

    Exr - George Champlin Mason, Jr. (nephew)

CHANDLER, Amos S.   E-1821   pr 2-p 207, 465
                                                 pr 3-p 341
    Admr - George Bowen   Waterford Twp.

CHAPMAN, Asahel   E-1832   pr 4-p 603, 604
                                                 pr 5-p 213
    Admr - Wheeler Chapman   Fearing Twp.

*CHAPMAN, Ezra A.   G-1845   pr 7-p 271
      Guardian - Benjamin F. Palmer

CHAPMAN, Hezekiah   E-1850   pr 8-p 473, 475, 509, 539
                                                 pr 9-p 457
      widow - Martha Chapman   Salem Twp.
      minor child - Mary

      Admr - David Ward

CHAPMAN, Jonathan   E-1820   pr 2-p 196, 244
      Admr - Levi Chapman   Fearing Twp.

CHAPMAN, Levi   W-1853   pr 9-p 447
      wife - Pheby   B-99
      brother - Simeon Chapman   Fearing Twp.
      Exrs - John Collins & Thomas F. Stanley

CHAPMAN, Selden   W-1840   pr 6-p 40, 91
      wife - Elizabeth   Fearing Twp.
      daus - Nancy S., Elizabeth A., Louisa M.,
            & Julia F.
      son - Oren S. (under age)

      Execx - wife, Elizabeth

CHAPPELL, Julius   E-1824   pr 3-p 184
                                                 pr 4-p 124
      Admx - Anna Chappell   Warren Twp.

CHAPPELL, Julius   E-1846   pr 7-p 373, 378
      Admr - John Clark   pr 8-p 153

CHEADLE, Asa   E-1837   pr 5-p 395
                                                 pr 6-p 33
      widow - Sally Cheadle   Roxbury Twp.
      children - unnamed
      Admr - Samuel Rogers

CHEADLE, Cyrus   W- 1850   pr 8-p 405
      wife -   Wesley Twp.
      son - Peter; other children, unnamed
      Exrs - Peter Cheadle & S. W. Smith

CHEEVER, Joshua   E-1790   pr 1-p 1, 4
      Admr - William Burnham (a creditor)   Marietta

CHERRY, John   E-1842   pr 6-p 404
    Admr - William Cherry   Fearing Twp.

CHILD, John   W-1826   pr 3-p 449
    of Warren, R. I. (Bristol Co.)
    where will proved 1819
    wife - Rosavilla Child
    children - John T. Child, Samuel Child, Nathan Child,
            Abigail M. Lewis, Rose A. Gardner

    Exrs - 3 sons - John T., Samuel & Nathan Child

CHUBB, Stephen   E-1790   pr 1-p 1, 4
    Admr - Capt. Josiah Monro (a creditor)   Marietta

CHURCHILL, Jacob   E-1823   pr 2-p 560
                                                    pr 3-p 22, 109
    widow & family, unnamed   pr 4-p 125
    Admr - L. D. Barker   Newport Twp.

CLARK, Ruth   E-1837   pr 5-p 390, 392
                                                    pr 6-p 8
    Admr - James Williamson   Marietta

CLARK, Seneca   E-1846   pr 7-p 331, 334, 342
                                                    pr 8-p 202
    Admrs - Augustin S. Clark & Theodore Devol   Waterford Twp.

CLARKE, John   W-1852   pr 9-p 238
                                                    B-48
    wife - Lorana   Marietta
    daus - Hulda Melissa Clark, Ester Ann Clark,
            Clarinda Jane Russel, Mary Curtis,
            Laurana Chamberlain
    sons - Timothy T. Clark (dec'd), Edward W. T. Clark

    Exr - Edward W. T. Clark

CLAY, Daniel   W-1824   pr 3-p 123, 180, 265, 291
    youngest son - Jonathan Clay   Salem Twp.
    eldest dau - Deborah Wharf

    Exr - Daniel Sanford

CLAYTON, Joseph   E-1829   pr 4-p 289, 291
    Admr - David Clayton   Wesley Twp.

CLINE, Philip   W-1852   pr 9-p 323
                                                    B-59
    wife - Elizabeth   Liberty Twp.
    son - George
    daus - not named

CLOGSTON, John Thomas   E-1846   pr 7-p 375, 379, 430
    widow & children, unnamed   Marietta Twp.
    Admr - James M. Booth

CLOUGH, Aaron   E-1823   pr 3-p 103, 104, 338
     Admr - Walter Curtis   Belpre Twp.

COBB, Samuel   W-1842   pr 6-p 340
     of Boston, Mass. where will probated, 1830

     wife - Sarah
     no sons or daus, but many legatees,
     nieces, nephews & others (not in this copy)

     Exr - Henderson Inches of Boston

COBURN, Asa   E-1797   pr 1-p 31, 34
     Admr - Robert Oliver, Esq.   Waterford Twp.

COGGESHALL, Daniel   E-1808   pr 1-p 94
                                                    Belpre Twp.

COGGESHALL, Daniel E.   E-1844   pr 7-p 27, 260
     Admr - John Shafer   Belpre Twp.

COGGESHALL, David   E-1844   pr 7-p 26, 259
     Admr - John Shafer   Belpre Twp.

COGSWELL, Eli Gilman   E-1817   pr 2-p38, 40, 92
     Admr - Eli Cogswell

COLE, Nathan   E-1817   pr 2-p 4, 50, 173, 272
     widow   Warren Twp.
     heirs receiving shares, 1822, are:
     Mary Jett, George Cole, Clarissa Hardy, Nathan
     Cole, Deborah Withee; Sampson Cole for himself
     & as gdn for Diana & Roenna Cole; John R. Cole
     & Levi Cole

     Admr - Sampson Cole

COLE, Philip   E-1831   pr 4-p 474, 485
     widow - Eunice   pr 5-p 75
     family (no names)   Warren Twp.

     Admr - J. P. Wightman
     Admx - Eunice Cole

COLES, Thomas   W-1846   pr 7-p 299
     of Providence, R. I. where will
     proved 1844

COLWELL, William   W-1852   pr 9-p 105, 154, 155, 171
     wife - Eve Ann Colwell   B-16
     heirs - not named   Watertown Twp.

     Exr - Ansel B. Ford

*CONKLIN, Mary et al   G-1837   pr 5-p 377
     Heirs of Richard Conklin of New York City
     dec'd 1832

     Petition by Gdn. to sell land in Fearing Twp.
     Washington County, Ohio for minors, Mary,
     Cornelia B., George W. H., Alanson H. &
     Antoinette Conklin
     also, he left a son - William H. Conklin,
     now 21 & wife - Mary

     Guardian - William Hughs of Williamsburg, Kings Co., N. Y.

CONKRIGHT, Richard   E-1848   pr 8-p 217, 219, 231, 467
     widow - Harriet Conkright   Barlow Twp.
     son - Richard Conkright, Jr.

     Admr - Nathan Stanton

CONVERS, Benjamin   E-1790   pr 1-p 4
     late of Wolf Creek Settlement   Marietta

     Admx - Esther Convers, widow

COOK, Joseph   W-1824   pr 3-p 153, 213
     wife - Rhoda   Belpre
     sons - Bennett, John, Joseph, Barker, Lillingast,
            Pardon
     daus - Pheba Hewett, Nancy James, Sally Johnson,
            Bathsheba Foly, Prudence Spencer, Elizabeth
            Darling

     Admr - John Stone, as named exrs refused

COOK, Joseph, Jr.   E-1823   pr 2-p 471
                                                  pr 3-p 128, 297
     widow & 3 children - no names   Belpre

     Admx - Clarissa Cook

COOK, Samuel   W-1832   pr 4-p 602
     wife - Rebecca Cook   Fearing Twp.
     dau - Mary Noble
     other children - William Cook, Rebecca Cook

     Exrs - James Noble & wife, Rebecca Cook

COOK, Silas   W-1851   pr 8-p 547
     wife   Marietta
     sons - Charles A., George N., Milton N.
     grandson - Silas, son of Milton N. Cook of
                Centerville, Butler Co., Pa.

     Exr - not named

COOMES, Henry   E-1852   pr 9-p 248, 270
  widow - Mary   B-47
  2 minor children under 15   Marietta

  Admr - Thomas W. Ewart

*COON, Elizabeth et al   G-1849   pr 8-p 348
  (Sarah Ann, Adaline, Isaac, Absalom & Susannah)
  All minor children of Tobias Coon (E-1843)

  Guardian - Joshua Cunningham

COON, Tobias   E-1843   pr 7-p 1, 2
                   pr 8-p 279
  Admrs - New Meredith & Isaac Coon Liberty Twp.

COOPER, Elijah   E-1821   pr 2-p 221, 252
  widow - Deborah   pr 3-p 138
  Admr - William Thorniley   Marietta

COOPER, Elisha Sr.   E-1851   pr 9-p 25, 28, 56
  widow   Jolly Twp.

  Admr - James C. Cooper

COOPER, Hannah   W-1801   pr 1-p 45, 49
  grandchildren - Abner, Lemuel, Frederick, Charles, Belpre
         Jacob & Hannah Cooper

  Exr - Jeremiah Cooper

COOPER, Joseph   W-1830   pr 4-p 325, 366
  wife - Mary   pr 5-p 446
  sons - John, William & Joseph, Jr.   Waterford Twp.
  daus - Jane & Harriet

  Execx - widow, Mary Cooper (who mar. _____ Sharp;
     and served as Mary Sharp at settlement)

COPPOCK, Isaac   W-1843   pr 6-p 438, 475
  wife - Mary   pr 7-p 76, 140, 307
  legacies to Matilda Monroe, wife of John pr 8-p 422
   Monroe; Isaac Monroe, son of Matilda, Wesley Twp.
   when 21; Amos Merrill, a "young man I raised";
   also, to my sister, Rachel Morris (wife of
   Joshua Morris); to Mary Neptune, Elizabeth
   Pickering, Jr.; Rachel Morris, Jr.; Matilda
   Morris; to my nieces, Lydia Heald & Mary
   Emmons; also, to Alice Morris

  Exrs - Jacob L. Myers & William Wilson

COPPOCK, Jonathan   E-1839   pr 6-p 51
                   pr 7-p 191
  Admr - Thomas Emmons   Roxbury Twp.

CORNER, George   E-1845   pr 7-p 208, 210
    Admr - David C. Racer   Marietta Twp.

CORNS, Henry   E-1826   pr 4-p 17, 619
                                                  pr 5-p 26
    Admr - John Corns   Wesley Twp.

CORNS, William   E-1832   pr 4-p 586, 587
                                                  pr 5-p 139
    Admr - Jabish F. Palmer   Roxbury Twp.

CORP, Benjamin   W-1848   pr 8-p 178
    son - Benjamin Corp & his son Benjamin Corp   Aurelius Twp.
    dau - Margaret McFarland Corp
    son - John S. Corp and his wife Elizabeth
    Benjamin Corp Ogle, son of James & Jane Ogle
    Benjamin Corp Preston

    Exr - son, John S. Corp

CORP, Mary   E-1825   pr 4-p 110
    Admr - William Thorniley, then
    Admr de bonis non - J. Cotton

CORY, Thomas   E-1823   pr 2-p 413
                                                  pr 4-p 384
    Admr - Charles S. Cory   Roxbury Twp.

CORY, Thomas S.   E-1850   pr 8-p 386, 430
    widow - Lucy Ann   Marietta Twp.
    minor children: William W. Corey, Horatio L. Corey,
                     Alice Dodge Corey, Mary Frances Corey,
                     Osborn Cross Corey
    (note omitted near top - Cory also sp. COREY)

    Admrs - John O. Cram & Richard H. Dodge

COTTON, Dr. John   E-1847   pr 7-p 583, 591
    widow & child, unnamed   pr 8- p 406
    dau - Susan B. Bullard   pr 9-p181
                                                  Marietta
    Admr - Dr. Josiah D. Cotton, son

COUNTANT, John Lewis   E-1793   pr 1-p 12
    Admr - Francis D'Hebecourt of Gallipolis   Gallipolis

COVEY, Cautious C.   E-1852   pr 9-p 321, 345, 356
    widow - Mary A.   B-55
    3 minor children   Marietta
    Admx - Mary A. Covey

COVEY, James   E-1847   pr 7-p 589
    Admx - wife, Eliza Covey

COVEY, Kingsbury   W-1840   pr 6-p 84, 133, 348

wife - Mary   Lawrence Twp.
sons - William, Benet & Kingsbury Covey
daus - mentioned but not named

Execx - Mary Covey, wife

CRAFT, Deborah   W-1838   pr 5-p 508
      pr 6-p 48, 86
Legatees number 14 - include bro. Richard   Fearing Twp.
      Smith, and many others whose relation is
      not explained

Admr - Underhill Lynch

*CRAM, John Oliver   G-1830   pr 4-p 339, 340, 341
      Jonathan Augustus
      Jacob

Three sons of Jonathan Cram

Guardian - Oliver Dodge

CRAM, Jonathan   E-1821   pr 2-p 246
      pr 3-p 392, 469, 481
widow - Sally (later mar. John Green -   pr 4-p 229
      26 Jan., 1826)   Marietta
children - Rebecca, John Oliver, Jonathan
      Augustus & Jacob Cram, all minors

Admx - Sally Cram, widow

CRANE, Ezra   E-1822   pr 2- 393, 394
      pr 3-p 127, 467
Admr - Ezekiel Deming   pr 4-p 32
      Marietta

CRANE, Miles   E-1821   pr 2-p 217, 467

Admr - John Gates, Jr.   Marietta

CRAVEN, Hiram   W-1852   pr 9-p 108, 189
      B-20
wife - Hannah   Wesley Twp.
children - Amy, Ezra, Manson, Calvin
      and John Craven; Loucinda Steinbrook,
      Ibu Harris

Exr - Thompson Walker

CRAWFORD, George   W-1849   pr 8-p 273
      Marietta Twp.
wife - Catharine
daus - Hannah Jane Crawford, Margareth Eliza
      Brown, Mary Ann Cline
son - John L. Crawford

Exr - wife, Catharine Crawford

CRAWFORD, John   E-1807   pr 1-p 128, 186
      Salem Twp.
Admr - Thomas Stanley

CRAWFORD, John   E-1852   pr 9-p 271, 278
    Admrs - William H. Crawford & Levi Barber   B-46
                                           Harmar

CRAWFORD, Joseph B.   E-1852   pr 9-p 271, 277, 278
    widow - Martha F.   B-46
    minor ch - Sue S., Francina   Harmar

    Admr - William H. Crawford

CRAWFORD, William   W-1843   pr 6-p 464
    wife - Sophronia Crawford   Salem Twp.
    children - not named

    Exr - wife, Sophronia, with brothers, Robert
        & John Crawford to assist

CREAMER, George   E-1852   pr 9-p 208
    late of Wheeling, Va.   B-36, 83
    widow - Drusilla   Newport
    minor children - Elizabeth, Christianna, Caroline

    Admr - Peter Snyder

CROSS, Waid   W-1819   pr 2-p 156, 176, 272
    son - Lucius Cross, land in Conn. inherited   pr 3-p 302
        from father, Peter Cross   Marietta
    wife - Bridget - Ohio lands with son, Lucius

    Execx - Bridget Cross (who mar. 2nd John Brough,
         3-21-1822, and died abt. July 1822)
    Admr de bonis non 1. Davidson Murray
                  2. Caleb Emerson

CULVER, John   E-1808   pr 1-p 106, 107
    widow - mentioned but not named   Belpre Twp.

CULVER, Levi   W-1836   pr 5-p 318
    wife - Nancy Culvert   pr 6-p 9
    sons by first wife: Isaac & Isaiah   Adams Twp.
    sons by 2nd wife, Nancy: William, John & Asa
    daus - Hannah Hinline; Elizabeth Carlin; Lucinda Dain;
        Nancy Culvert
    servant boy - Jesse Hissington, to live with and serve
               youngest son, Asa Culver

    Exr - Enoch Rector

CUNNINGHAM, Philip   E-1823   pr 2-p 353
    Admr - John Cunningham   Marietta

*CURRY, Jane   G-1842   pr 7-p 62
    Guardian - George Curry

CURTIS, Barnabas   E-1847   pr 7-p 621
    Admr - Samuel B. Robinson   pr 8- P 1, 41, 129, 352
                                              Waterford Twp.

CURTIS, Eleazer   E-1802   pr 1-p 53, 54
    Admx - Eunice Curtis   Belpre Twp.

CURTIS, Mrs. Eunice   E-1815   pr 1-p 284, 285, 305b
    Admrs - Eleazer S. Curtis & Walter Curtis   (second page labelled 305)
                                                Belpre Twp.

CURTIS, Jason R.   E-1834   pr 5-p 200, 242, 472
    widow - Mary Curtis   Marietta Twp.
    heirs - William F., Charles A., Sarah J.,
               James D., Mary B., Adeliza and Lucy
               G. Curtis, all minors

    Admx - Mary Curtis, widow

CURTISS, John   E-1828   pr 4-p 238, 240, 424, 466
    no widow mentioned   Barlow Twp.
    7 children: Paul B. of age by 1830;
       6 minors: Hiram (1); Thomas Weston (2);
       Harriet (3); Catherine (4); George (5);
       guardian, Abner Woodruff, Jr.; & John
       (6) with gdn., Ephraim Palmer

    Admr - Jabish F. Palmer

CUSHING, Nathaniel   E-1814   pr 1-p 276, 288, 289
    Admrs - N. S. Cushing & Dan'l Goodno   pr 2-p 31, 88, 89
                                                  Belpre Twp.

CUSHING, Samuel   E-1817   pr 2-p 12, 14, 28, 32
    widow - Bathsheba (who mar. Benjamin Beedle   Waterford Twp.
           of Hocking Co., 29 Dec., 1818)
    children - only Samuel, Jr. named

    Admx - Bathsheba Cushing
    Admr - Sam Cushing, Jr.

CUSHING, Samuel, Jr.   E-1823   pr 3-p 110, 111, 325, 434
    widow - Almira Cushing, mar. _____ Beach   Waterford Twp.
    only child - minor, Charles Cushing

    Admr - Obadiah Scott

CUTLER, William   W-1838   pr 5-p 476
    of Portsmouth, N. H.   Rockingham Co.
    where will proved, 1817)
    father - Annai Ruhamah Cutler
    mother

    Exrs - Daniel Cutler, bro., & Daniel R. Rogers,
         brother-in-law, named in will

DALLIEZ, Maria Josephine   W-1800   pr 1-p 37, 40
    Legatees: John Vandenbenden, son of Merthias   Gallipolis
    Vandenbenden; single women: Ange Mick &
    Alexandriene Maguet; Mrs. Davous, wife of
    Francis Davous; Lydia Safford, child of
    Robert & Catherine Safford

    Exr - Robert Safford

DANA, Benjamin   W-1838   pr 5-p 511
    wife - Sally   pr 6-p 201
    son - John Winchester Dana   Waterford Twp
    daus - Eliza Fearing, Eunice C. Dana, Charlotte
        P. Allen & Caroline Dawes

    Exrs - John Winchester Dana & Henry Fearing
        (son & son-in-law)

DANA, Edmund B.   E-1836   pr 5-p 320, 442, 471
    widow - Jerusha Dana   Union Twp.

    Admx - Jerusha Dana

DANA, Eunice   E-1842   pr 6-p 356
    Legacies: to Dr. John Allen, Caroline Dawes, pr 8-p 462
    Henry Fearing & J. W. Dana (these are   Waterford Twp.
    bros-in-law, sister & brother); and (she
    is probable dau of Benjamin Dana.)

    Admr - Boylston Shaw

DANA, John W.   E-1850   pr 8-p 432, 575
    minor children: Sarah Marietta Dana &   pr 9-p 464
                     Caroline D. Dana

    Admr - Boylston Shaw

*DANA, Lucy Mariah   G-1840   pr 6-p 126
    (bro. seems to be Thomas B. Dana)   pr 7-p 51

    Guardian - R(ichard) D. Hollister

DANA, Luther   E-1814   pr 1-p 266, 316
    widow - not named   pr 2-p 469
    Stephen Dana is guardian of the heirs   Newport Twp.

    Admr - William Dana

DANA, Sally   E-1847   pr 7-p 452
    legatees: John Allen & J. W. Dana   pr 8-p 460
    Admr - Boylston Shaw   Waterford Twp.

                              Washington County, Ohio Probate -31-

DANA, Stephen   E-1834   pr 5-p 187, 193, 468, 500
     widow - Elizabeth M. Dana   pr 9-p 593
     pr 9-p 593-petition to sell land to   Newport Twp.
            benefit grand children

     Admx - Elizabeth M. Dana

*DANA, Thomas B.   G-1840   pr 6-p 128
     (sister is prob. Lucy Mariah Dana but   pr 7-p 49
      father's name not given)

     Guardian - R. D. Hollister

DANA, William, Sr.   E-1810   pr 1-p 190, 262, 263
     Admr - Edmund B. Dana   pr 4-p 255
                                                Belpre Twp.

DANA, William   W-1852   pr 9-p 146, 333, 398
     wife - Maria   B-20, 60, 63
     heirs, named in petition (p 398) as Elizabeth   Newport Twp.
        McCracken, Francis Archibold, Mary B. Dustan,
        Grace D. Ewart, Charles Dana, Joseph Dana Clarke;
        also, Joseph Dana Williams, B. Dana, Dorcas I.,
        Asa M., Constant Ann, Nancy M., Isabel W. and
        Henry L. Dana

     Admr - with will annexed - Melvin Clark

DANA, William P.   W-1853   pr 9-p 593
     widow - Ann   Wills I-p 3
     4 minor ch - Charles, Mary, Ann   B-111
            and Susan S. whose guardian   Marietta
            is Stephen A. Dana

     Exr - Luther D. Dana

DANIELSON, Timothy E.   E-1813   pr 1-p 241, 249, 251
                                                Marietta

DARROW, Russell   E-1815   pr 1-p 282
                                                Deerfield Twp.
                                              (now in Morgan Co.)

DAVIS, Dudley   E-1825   pr 3-p 403, 405
     widow - allowance for year's support   Salem Twp.

     Admrs - Frederick Davis & Marvil Davis

DAVIS, Dudley W.   E-1849   pr 8-p 316, 317, 561
     Heirs are Mindwell R. Davis, Marvil Davis, Jr.,   pr 9 -p 165
        Elect.a Davis & the wife of John   Waterford Twp.
        Tarbill, admr.

     Admr - John Tarbill

DAVIS, Hezekiah   E-1816   pr 1-p 297, 298

DAVIS, Jonas   E-1795   pr 1-p 15
  Admr - Isaac Peirce   Belpre Twp.

DAVIS, Nathaniel   E-1790   pr 1-p 5, 8
  Admr - Benjamin Tupper, Esq.   Marietta

DAVIS, Nehemiah   E-1836   pr 5-p 326
  Allowance for young children   pr 6-p 2, 7
                       Barlow Twp.
  Admr - John Hougland

DAVIS, Thomas G.   W-1828   pr 4-p 214, 462, 540
  father - Stephen Davis   pr 5-p 506
  widow - Mary, who had his son, George Thomas Marietta
     Davis, posthumously, and married
     2nd, John Eadie (or Eddy)

  Admr - Augustus Stone

DAVIS, William   W-1843   pr 6-p 465
  wife - Sarah Davis   pr 7-p 3, 22, 147
  son - Jesse Davis   Adams Twp.
  daus - Sarah & Sophia Davis
  other children not named, except Asa as exr,
    but he did not serve

  Execx - wife, Sarah

DAVIS, William, Jr.   E-1830   pr 4-p 449, 455
  widow & heirs   pr 5-p 209
                       Adams Twp.
  Admx - Jerusha Davis

DEAN, Elizabeth   E-1825   pr 3-p 463, 560

  Heirs - Ebenezer Dean, Frances Dean & Balch Dean,
     named in petition to sell land, drawn in
     name of Jonathan Dean

  Admr - Josiah Dean of Dedham, Mass.

  (Note omitted above: Elizabeth Dean was from
  Dedham, Mass.)

DELANO, Amos   E-1817   pr 2-p 48, 74, 91
  Admx - Cynthia Delano   Warren Twp.

DELANO, Cornelius   E-1824   pr 3-p 223, 462
  Heirs - Henry Delano, Elizabeth Broderick,   Belpre Twp.
     Jane Armstrong, Clarinda Delano,
     not found in Washington County, Ohio

  Admr - Asa Morey (or Mory)

DELANO, Thomas   W-1834   pr 5-p 114, 145, 260
    wife - Cynthia   Warren Twp.
    other legatees are - Julia Ann & Lucy Angeline
        Delano, heirs of Amos Delano, dec'd
    Exrs - wife, Cynthia and Jasper Needham

DELAVERGNE, Edward M.   E-1844   pr 7-p 91
    widow - Harriet   Marietta
    Admr - George W. De LaVergne

DELONG, Jonathan   E-1815   pr 1-p 274, 275, 289, 314
    widow - not named   Salem Twp.
    heirs - ten others (including admr, but they
        are not named
    Admr - Isaac H. DeLong

DEMING, Abigal   E-1823   pr 3-p 70, 218
                                                            pr 5-p 156, 371
    Admr - Lucius Cross   pr 6-p 153 (1841)
                                                            Marietta

DENNIT, John   W-1823   pr 2-p 443
    Brothers & Sisters - Reuben, Lydia, Abigail,   pr 3-p 73
        Anna, Samuel, Unice, Hannah, Moses   Waterford Twp.
    Friend - Hugh Allison, Jr.
    Exr - Hugh Allison, Jr.

DEVEREUX, Alanson   E-1828   pr 4-p 141
    Admr - Joseph Devereux   Waterford Twp.

DEVIN, Michael   E-1822   pr 2-p 258, 261, 273
    widow - Elizabeth Devin   pr 3-p 300
    Admrs - Thomas Devin & Michael Devin   Waterford Twp.

DEVOL, Allen   E-1845   pr 7-p 217, 222, 320, 477
    widow - Rachel   Waterford Twp.
    Admr - Simeon M. Devol

DEVOL, Allen, Jr.   E-1847   pr 8-p 90
    Admr - Frederick C. Davis   Waterford Twp.

*DEVOL, Charles H.   G-1850   pr 8-p 424
    Guardian - A. T. Nye

DEVOL, Cook   W-1834   pr 5-p 142, 203, 206,
    Wife - Patience   258, 410
    Children - sons - Dalphon & Grovenor   Waterford Twp.
              daus - Balinda & Martha Jane (youngest)
    Exrs - wife, Patience & son, Dalphon Devol

DEVOL, Daniel   E-1847   pr 8-p 106, 587, 593
   Son - Daniel, of full age   B-1, 3, 4, 17
   Minor children - Hamilton, Rachel Elizabeth,   Waterford Twp.
      Sarah, Caroline, Ann Eliza & Hannah
   At settlement in 1851, Rachel Elizabeth
      Devol was mar. to _____ Farnesworth

   Admr - Daniel M. Sprague

DEVOL, Francis   E-1846   pr 7-p 377, 416, 419
   Widow   pr 8-p 244
   1 minor child   Union Twp.

   Admr - John Crawford

DEVOL, George W.   E-1841   pr 6-p 227, 243, 397
   Widow
   2 children under 14 yrs.

   Admx - Mary Anne Devol

DEVOL, Gilbert   W-1824   pr 3-p 151, 225, 261, 365,416
   Wife - Anne   pr 4-p 124
   daus - Sarah Hinckley, Priscilla White,   Waterford Twp.
      Polly McClure, Barsheba Beedle
   heirs of dec'd sons - Wanton Devol, Jonathan
      Devol & Gilbert Devol, Jr.
   pr 4-p 124 is a petition to sell land and named many
      more heirs, including many grandchildren

   Admr - Samuel Beach, Esq.

DEVOL, Gilbert, Jr.   E-1812   pr 1-p 204, 206, 234, 249,
   Widow - Rachel   pr 2-p 16   265, 283
   children - not named; but see petition to   Marietta
      sell land of Gilbert, Sr., in
      pr 4-p 124

   Admr - James Whitney

DEVOL, Isaac   W-1852   pr 9p 110
   wife - Elizabeth   Adams Twp.
      at her death legacies to Charles Devol;
      to Elizabeth and Esabel Devol, heirs of
      George Devol and balance to
   daus - Rebecca Spooner, Patience Morse and
   sons - Abner, Richmond, Charles M. Devol

*DEVOL, John Bennet   G-1851   pr 8-p 572
   Adaline, Simeon M., Augusta &
   Alexander C., children of Allen Devol

   Guardian - Augustus W. Sprague
   Probable mother, Edith Devol was paid for support
   new guardian for Augusta & Alexander C. is S. M. Sprague

DEVOL, Jonathan   E-1809   pr 1-p 185, 187, 208, 209
    Widow - Clarissa, mar. 2nd, Charles Sullivan   233, 234, 240, 264,2
      of Muskingum County, 8 Sept., 1812   pr 3-p 218, 328
    Admr - Luther Dana   Waterford Twp.
    2nd Admr - William Gray (dec'd 1812)
    Admr. de bonis non - B(enjamin) F. Stone

DEVOL, Capt. Jonathan   W-1824   pr 3-p 156, 226
    Oldest son - Charles; 2nd son, Barker; Francis   pr 7-p 263
    dau - Mariah Barker   Union Twp.
    heirs of dec'd dau. Sally McFarling

    Exr - son, Francis Devol
    Admr de bonis non - Benjamin F. Stone

*DEVOL, Martha Jane   G-1837   pr 5-p 411
    (dau of Cook Devol, dec'd)   pr 7-p 181 (1845)
    heir to ¼ of father's estate, after widow's
      dower taken;
    Martha J. was only age 6 in 1837, so was
      age 15 at settlement in 1845

    Guardian - Stephen Devol

DEWEES, William   W-1852   pr 9-p 162, 209, 210
    wife - "Debbie"   B-33
    daus - Mary Dewees, Sarah Doudna   Wesley Twp.
    son - Isaac, dec'd

    Admr with will annexed - Elijah Fawcett

DEXTER, John Singer   W-1847   pr 7-p 466
    of Cumberland R. I. (Providence Co.)
    where will proved 1844

    Many heirs

    Exrs - John Pearce Dexter & Frederick P. Eddy
        (son)

DICKERSON, Sarah   W-1840   pr 6-p 85, 134
    (dau of Thomas Dickerson)

    Execx - sister, Rebecca Dickerson

DICKERSON, Thomas   W-1827   pr 4-p 62, 106, 107, 334
    daus - Rebecca & Sarah   Grandview Twp.
    sons - Thomas & Joseph

    Exr - Joseph Dickerson

DICKEY, Eliza   E-1848   pr 8-p 230, 297
    (one of 13 children of Solomon Dickey)   Union Twp.

    Admx - Margaret Dickey, widow of Solomon Dickey

DICKEY, Solomon   W-1835   pr 5-p 221, 255, 504
    wife - Margaret   B-125
    children - not named here   Union Twp.

    Execx - wife, Margaret

DILLEY, Joseph   E-1846   pr 7-p 315, 322, 325
    Admr - Bial Stedman   Belpre Twp.

DILLON, Zachariah   E-1850   pr 8-p 524, 527, 528
    widow - Rosannah Dillon
    minor children - Eliza, Jane, Mary, Elizabeth,
                     Sarah Ellen, William Henery & David

    Admr - Daniel Davis at Lowell

*DOAN, Archibald S. et al   G-1831   pr 4-p 573
    (Elbridge G., Henrietta Maria, Juliann &   pr 5-p 233
     Caroline Joanna)
    Petition of these children of Orgillous Doan
    to sell land, with each of five children
    entitled to 1/7 of same, subject to dower
    of Jerusha Hill, wife of Harry Hill, & formerly
    widow of Orgillious Doan, by

    Guardian - Samuel Shipman

DOAN, Orgillous   E-1823   pr 3-p 74, 80
    widow - Jerusha Doan, mar. 2nd the   pr 4-p 253, 628
            admr. Harry Hill   Salem Twp.
            (see also petition of 5 children to
            sell land by their gdn., Samuel Shipman)
            (pr 4-p 573 & pr 5-p 233)

    Admr - Harry Hill

*DODGE, Andrew   G-1818   pr 2-p 103, 205
    (son of John Dodge, dec'd, 1805)
    Accts. of 1st gdn., Charles H. Martin
    who lives in Newark & is being discharged.
    New gdn. to be Sidney Dodge & admrs of
    John Dodge estate.

    1st Gdn. - Charles H. Martin
    2nd Gdn. - Sidney Dodge

DODGE, John   E-1805   pr 1-p 81, 114, 268
    widow - Catherine Dodge   pr 2-p 102, 104
    p. 268, the partition of lands gives the   Waterford Twp.
    children - John & William M. Dodge; Susanna M.
    Baker; Sydney, Solomon, Polly & Andrew Dodge

    Admrs - John Dodge & Isaac Baker

```
DODGE, John                    E-1854              pr 9-p 531, 553, 602, 625
    Legal heirs - Israel S. Dodge, Sidney Dodge,   B-163,175, 187, 339, 422
      Patterson O. Dodge, Collenia N.              Beverly
      Robinson; Samuel H. & John H.
      Brooks, minors; William M. Dodge,
      Eliza A. Glass, William M. Brooks;
      Henry & Eliza McQuire, infants

    Admrs - Patterson O. Dodge, Samuel B. Robinson

DODGE, Nathaniel               W-1838              pr 5-p 478, 521, 544, 556
    daus - Sally Greene, Polly Tilton of Exeter,   pr 6-p 197, 394
      N.H.; heirs of Jonathan Cram & of            Marietta Twp.
      Daniel P. Bosworth; children of dec'd
      dau, Rebecca Stone
    son - Oliver Dodge & his children: Wallace &
      Mary W. Dodge; also, grandchildren: Nathaniel
      & Dudley Tilton

    Exrs - Daniel P. Bosworth & Richard H. Dodge

DODGE, Oliver                  E-1817              pr 2-p 42, 201
    widow                                          Adams Twp.
    family

    Admx - Anna Dodge

*DODGE, Polly                  G-1818              pr 2-p 102
    (dau of John Dodge, dec'd 1805)
    Accts. of 1st gdn., Charles H. Martin, who lives
    in Newark & is being discharged;
    new gdn. to be Sidney Dodge; also mention of
    Isaac Baker & John Dodge, admrs of John Dodge estate,
    late of Waterford

    1st gdn - Charles H. Martin
    2nd gdn - Sidney Dodge

DOLAN, William                 W-1839              pr 5-p 537, 588
    wife - Catharine Dolan                         pr 6-p 253
    sons - William, Jr. & Thomas Dolan             Waterford Twp.

    Exrs - sons, William, Jr. & Thomas Dolan

DORR, Matthew                  E-1802              pr 1-p 48, 51
    Admr - Edmund Dorr                             Middletown Twp.
                                                   (now part of Athens Co.)

DOUGLAS, John                  W-1830              pr 4-p316
    (of Plainfield, Windham Co., Conn. where will was
    probated, 1824)
    wife - Pamela and future children, if any; also,
           sisters, nephews, nieces not listed here

    Exrs - Joseph Eaton & Henry Sabin

                                 Washington County, Ohio Probate  -38-
```

DOUGLAS, William   W-1839   pr 6-p 20
    (of Plainfield, Windham Co., Conn where will
    probated 1811)
    mentions 4 living sisters, 1 dec'd sister;
    1 bro John; 7 nieces & nephews; no wife or ch
    of his own

DRAKE, Enoch   E-1841   pr 6-p 242
    widow   Salem Twp.
    7 children under age of 15 yrs.

    Admr - John P. Hall

DROWN, John   E-1815   pr 1-p 292, 293, 303
    widow - Mary   pr 2-p 3
    family   Marietta
    Admr - George Dunlevy

DROWN, John Jr.   E-1825   pr 3-p 289
    His late Gdn. was Mary Chadwick, formerly Marietta
    Mary Drown
    other heirs mentioned, not named

    Admr - George Dunlevy

DROWN, Notley   E-1831   pr 4-p 490
    widow   Marietta
    4 children

    Admr - W. Knox

DROZ, Peter   E-1795   pr 1-p 14, 22
    Admr - Lewis Violette   Gallipolis

DRURY, Abraham   W-1841   pr 6-p 252
    wife - Catharine Drury   pr 8-p 32
    children - Ulmer, Ambroes, Annis, Daniel, Eliza, Waterford Twp
            Abijah, Isaac Drury & Levina D. Fry

    Admr - S. B. Robinson

DRURY, Daniel F.   E-1843   pr 7-p 38, 39
    Admr - S. B. Robinson   pr 8-p 33
                                              Waterford Twp.

DUCHALLARD, Peter   E-1795   pr 1-p 14
    Admr - John Gilbert Petit, Esquire   Gallipolis Twp.

DUDLEY, Charles E.   W-1845   pr 7-p 176
    (of Albany, N.Y. where will was probated, 1840)
    wife - Vlondina Dudley

    Exr - Thomas W. Olcott

DUFUR, David   E-1818   pr 2-p 129, 130, 256
   widow   Belpre Twp.
   Admr - George Dana

DUNBAR, Samuel   E-1823   pr 2-p 479
   heirs - not named   pr 3-p 448, 480
   Admr - Francis Devol   Union Twp.

DUNCAN, Mary   E-1829   pr 4-p 294
   heirs mentioned, not named   Marietta
   one son, Valentine Duncan, died, 1826
   Admr - Caleb Emerson

DUNCAN, Robert G.   E-1823   pr 2-p 553
   heirs, John Duncan & Howell L. L. Duncan,   pr 4-p 174, 288, 299, 311
     resident in Va.;   Marietta
   Ann Cole, minor (by her father & gdn.,
     Sampson Cole);
   Nancy Hoff, wife of Enoch Hoff of Marietta;
   Sally Cole, wife of admr Levi Cole;
   also, the right of Valentine Duncan, dec'd
   Admrs - Levi Cole & Wm Slocomb

DUNCAN, Valentine   E-1826   pr 4-p 10, 294
   Admr - C(aleb) Emerson

DUNHAM, Daniel   E-1791   pr 1-p 5, 13, 17
   son - Jonathan Dunham   Belpre Twp.
   dau - _____ Wright
   Admr - Bathsheba Dunham, widow of dec'd

DUNHAM, Jonathan   E-1823   pr 2-p 483, 486
   widow - Jerusha Dunham   pr 4-p 38
   Admr - Amos Dunham   Warren Twp.

*DUNLEVY, David B.   G-1846   pr 7-p 393
   Guardian - John Crawford

DUNLEVY, George   E-1837   pr 5-p387, 516
   wife - Eliza   pr 6-p 4, 126
   4 children under age 15   Marietta
   Admx - Eliza Dunlevy

*DUNLEVY, George W.   G-1846   pr 7-p 394
   Guardian - John Crawford

*DUNLEVY, Harriet   G-1846   pr 7-p 393
   Guardian - John Crawford

```
DUNN, Hugh                      E-1829               pr 4-p 326, 327
    widow - Mary                                     Wesley Twp.

    Admrs - Mary Dunn & William C. Dunn


DUNSMOORE, Phineas              E-1823               pr 3-p 23, 24, 141
    wife - Polly                                     pr 4-p 35
    son - Horace, above age 21;                      Wesley Twp.
    other children - Abner G., Mary K., Hiel,
                     Lucius P., Adeline &
                     Daniel N. Dunsmoore

    Admrs - Polly Dunsmoore, widow &
            Horace Dunsmoore, son


DURANT, Nathan                  E-1825               pr 3-p 536
    (also DURRANT)                                   pr 4-p 25, 69, 297
    1st Admr - Wm Durant                             Marietta Twp.
    Admr de bonis non - Timothy Buell


DURFEE, George W.               E-1823               pr 2-p 540
                                                     Union Twp.


DURKEE, Doctor Silas            E-1813               pr 1-p 239, 254
    widow                                            Waterford Twp.
    family

    Admr - Marvel Starlin
    Admx - Eleanor Durkee


DUSTIN, William                 E-1850               pr 8-p 524, 525
    Widow - Eunice Dustin                            pr 9-p 114
    10 heirs - John Dustin; Eunice (wife of Leonard  Barlow Twp.
               Hartshorn); Mary Dustin; George W.
               Dustin; John Vincent's wife; S. L.
               Gould's wife; Emily Swan; William Dustin;
               L. W. Dustin; Mighill Dustin (his share)

    Admr - John Dustin


DUTTON, Joseph                  E-1841               pr 6-p257, 403
    widow                                            Aurelius Twp.

    Admr - Daniel Davis


DUVALL, Mareen                  W-1852               pr 9-p 206
    wife                                             B-42, 372
    children by 1st wife - not named                 Independence Twp.
    grandsons - William Blakiston Duvall, Ephraim
                Taylor Duvall
    dau - Mary A. Green

    Exr - Joseph A. Duvall (son)
```

```
DUVERGER, Francis            W-1797           pr 1-p 23, 25
                                              Gallipolis Twp.
    Brothers & sisters all of France:
    Stephen Duverger, Anthony Duverger, &
    Martha Duverger

    Exr - John Gilbert Petit, Esq. of Gallipolis


DYAR, John, Sr.              W-1833           pr 5-p 54, 93, 496
    (also DYER)                               Union Twp.

    wife - Sally
    sons - Joseph B., John, Jr., Benjamin Franklin
            & Albert Dyar
    daus - Sarah Otis; Esther Ann Ridgway; & Harriet Dyar;
    also, heirs of dec'd dau, Mary Jenkins

    Execx - wife - Sally


DYAR, John, Jr.              E-1835           pr 5-p 267, 321, 448
    widow - Rosanna D. Dyar                   Union Twp.

    Admrs - Rosanna D. Dyar & J. B. Dyar


DYE, Daniel,                 E-1853           pr 9-p 453, 547
    widow - Nancy                             B-87b, 164
    minor child - Theodore A. Dye             Grandview Twp.
    ch. of full age - Terissa McMahan (wife of Wm. L.),
                      Angeline Dye

    Admrs - William L. McMahan, Nancy Dye


DYE, Daniel H.               E-1836           pr 5-p 364, 556
                                              pr 6-p 11
                                              Lawrence Twp.


DYE, John                    W-1823           pr 2-p 388
    wife - Elizabeth         (proved, May)    Lawrence Twp.
    6 sons - Amos, John, Thomas, Samuel, Jonathan
            & Ezekiel
    5 daus - Jenny, Mary, Sarah, Elizabeth & Patience

    Exrs - sons - John & Samuel


DYE, John, Jr.               W-1823           pr 2-p 439
    wife - Hannah            (proved Nov.)    Lawrence Twp.
    6 sons - John Washington Dye; Daniel Hoff Dye;
            Andrew Jackson Dye; Thomas; Moffet; &
            Samuel, a minor
    3 daus - Susannah Peirce; Emma & Hannah Dye

    Exrs - Thomas & Moffet Dye
```

DYE, Jonathan   W-1851   pr 9-p 69, 95, 108, 486
    Wife - Fanny   B-38, 112
    sons - Thomas, Amos, Alexander, Samuel 3rd   Lawrence Twp.
    daus - Matilda Wilgus, Elizabeth Dye, Jane Dye
    bro - Amos Dye

    Exr - Thomas Dye

*DYER, Augusta R.   G-1851   pr 8-p 569

    minor heir of John Dyer,(Jr.), dec'd,
    now Augusta R. Huggins

    Guardian - John Crawford

*DYER, John W.   G-1851   pr 8-p 567

    minor heir of John Dyer (Jr.) dec'd
    whose widow was Rosanna D. Dyar
    and is now Rosanna D. Selby

    Guardian - John Crawford

EDDY, Frederick A.   W-1848   pr 8-p 104
    (of Boston, Mass. where will proved, 1847)

    Legatees are: Uncle John P. Dexter; Eliza Whipple,
                   wf of John G. Whipple of Providence,
                   R.I.; Mrs. Charlotte Leach, widow;
                   Nathaniel Greene of N.Y. & Joel Scott
                   of Boston

    Exr - Joel Scott

EDGERTON, Luther   E-1823   pr 3-p 88, 303
    Family got support for 1 yr, but no names given   Marietta

    Admr - William H. Shipman

EDLESTON, Jarvis   W-1850   pr 8-p 517
    wife - Mary   Harmar
    "to all my children except dau Mary, wife of Thomas H.
    Wells, who has been provided for by property from
    her mother, my 1st wife"

    Execx - wife - Mary Edleston

EDWARDS, David   E-1848   pr 8-p 180, 267, 271
    wife - Rachel   Ludlow Twp.
    sons - James R., Charles H., A. Whittlesey &
           Bazelle (or Bazzele) Edwards
    daus - Mary B. Scott, Prisla Bloomer &
           Elizabeth P. Edwards

    Exrs - wife - Rachel & Alexander Bell

ELDER, James   E-1847   pr 7-p 613, 615
    wife - Sarah Elder   pr 8-p 41, 288
    minor children - Sarah Matilda & Isabella Elder   pr 8-p 600
    pr 8-p 600 gives accts by their gdn., James   Ludlow Twp.
    Rinard; also, for James & Henry Elder, their bros.

    Admr - Richard Scott

                              Washington County, Ohio Probate   -43-

ELLENWOOD, Benjamin   E-1826   pr 3-p 527, 529
    widow   pr 4-p 159
    Admr - Samuel Ellenwood   Belpre Twp.

ELLENWOOD, Isaac Q.   E-1847   pr 7-p 606,610
    2 minor children   pr 8-p 42, 289
    Admr - John Ellenwood   Belpre Twp.

ELLIS, Ephraim   W-1849   pr 8-p 275, 324, 325,
    daus - Susannah Hill, Mary Joy, Rosanna   330, 388
       Brokaw & Martha Shra(der?)   Roxbury Twp.
    sons - Levi, Ephraim C., Alfred, Isaac,
       Moses & John
    also, to heirs of Joel Ellis & to Thomas J. Ellis

    Admr - Alfred Ellis apptd.- since Levi declined to serve as exr

ELLIS, Henry   E-1852   pr 9-p 416, 450, 462, 492
    no widow or children   B-93
    heirs are - Benjamin Ellis of Knox Co., Ohio;   Grandview Twp.
              Martin Ellis of Champlin Co., N.Y.;
              Diana Burris, wife of Stinson Ellis
              & Stinson Ellis

    Admr - Silas Ellis (bro.)

ELLIS, Ira   W-1842   pr 6-p 377, 436
    wife & 5 heirs, all unnamed   Wesley Twp.
    also, legacy to Mary Ann Anderson if she remains
       in family

    Exr - Reuben Ellis, 2nd

ELLIS, John   E-1841   pr 7-p 261
    Admr - John D. Chamberlain

EMERSON, Caleb   W-1853   pr 9-p 384, 463
    wife - Mary   B-79
    son - William D.   Marietta
    Admr - Thomas W. Ewart

EMERSON, Ephraim   W-1834   pr 5-p 118
    heirs - William Dana Emerson &   Marietta
       Caleb Emerson

    Exr - Caleb Emerson

EMERSON, Ira   E-1837   pr 5-p 360, 505
    Admr - John D. Chamberlain   Watertown Twp.

EMMONS, Isaac   E-1800   pr 1-p 36
    Admr - William Skinner, a creditor   Marietta

EVANS, David   E-1842   pr 6-p 281
    widow   pr 7-p 185
    Admr - Caleb Emerson   Adams Twp.

EVERETT, David   E-1814   pr 1-p 265, 266
                                                       Marietta.

EWART. Robert K.   W-1852   pr 9-p 267, 275
    wife - Mary   B-55
    ch - Elizabeth J., Thomas   Grandview Twp.
    also mentioned little Lucy

    Admx - with will annexed - Mary Ewart (widow)

FAIRBROTHER, Henry   E-1836   pr 5-p 302
    widow   Aurelius Twp.
    child, not named

    Admx - Elizabeth Fairbrother

FAIRCHILD, Amos   E-1823   pr 3-p 84, 85, 86
    widow - Hannah   pr 4-p 306
    children of full age - Hiram, Erastus, Polly   Decatur Twp.
            (wife of Abel Dufur), Lucy (wife of
            Eli Gilbert, Jr.)
    minors - Daniel S., Levi, Joseph W., & Samuel A.

    Admr - David Fairchild

FAIRCHILD, Major   W-1795   pr 1-p 18, 19
    nephew - William Fairchild   Marietta
    children of sister - Ann Boler
    other legatees - Christian Burnham (wife of
    Wm Burnham of Marietta); Abel Rice

    named exrs refused, so apptd.
    Admr - Dr. Jabez True of Marietta

FARIS, Francis   E-1853   pr 9-p 466
    Admr - Matthew Faris   B-74
                                                       Warren Twp.

FARIS, William   E-1818   pr 2-p 113, 190
    Admr - William Faris, Jr.   Warren Twp.

FAYLES, Turpin   E-1793   pr 1-p 11, 18
    Admr - William Chambers of Mason Co., KY   Marietta
            (a creditor)

```
FEARING, Noah                W-1809              pr 1-p 171, 172
    wife - Rebeccah                              Marietta
    sons - Silas & Paul
    dau - Lucy Willis

    Exr - Paul Fearing (son)

FEARING, Paul                W-1822              pr 2-p 267, 346
    widow                                        Marietta
    dau - Lucy W. Mayberry
    son - Henry Fearing

    Exrs - Henry Fearing (son) & John P. Mayberry
        of Parkersburg, Va.

FEARING, Rodolphus           E-1838              pr 5-p 548
                                                 pr 6-p 87
    widow - Sarah Fearing                        Harmar-Marietta Twp.
    3 children

    Admr - John Crawford

FELCH, Ebenezer              E-1799              pr 1-p 36, 70
                                                 Newport Twp.
    Widow - Sarah Felch

    Admr - Dudley Woodbridge, Esq.

FELLSHAW, Samuel             E-1796              pr 1-p 19
                                                 Marietta
    Admr - Daniel Davis of Waterford

FERGUSON, Joshua             E-1825              pr 3-p 356
                                                 pr 4-p 247
    widow & family - no names                    Marietta Twp.

    Admr - Joseph Barker, Jr.

FIELDS, Samuel C.            E-1841              pr 6-p 255
                                                 pr 7-p 49, 488
    wife - Sally S. Fields (who died also in 1841)  Marietta Twp.
    son - Henry H. Fields

    Admx - Sally S. Fields (wife)
    Admr de bonis non - Henry H. Fields
    Third Admr - Jonas Moore (see pr 7-p 488)

FINCH, Asha                  E-1832              pr 4-p 550, 552
                                                 pr 5-p 140
    Admr - Reuben Finch                          Warren Twp.

FINCH, Lewis                 E-1831              pr 4-p 534, 536
                                                 pr 5-p 78
    widow & family - no names                    Warren Twp.
    Admr - R(euben) Finch

FISHER, (Col) Daniel         E-1824              pr 3-p 228, 230, 423
                                                 pr 4-p 196, 197
    Admr - George Dana                           pr 6-p 88
                                                 Belpre Twp.
```

```
*FLAGG, James               G-1793              pr 1-p 11
     Guardian apptd for James Flagg, minor
     at request of his mother, Editha Flagg
     Guardian not named

FLANDERS, Ezekiel           E-1849              pr 8-p 271
     Widow & children mentioned but no names    pr 9-p 355
                                                Fearing Twp
     Admr - Elisha Allen

FLANNERY, Samuel            E-1852              pr 9-p 120, 121, 172
     widow - Mary Flannery                      B-21, 296
     minor ch. - James, Sarah, Mary Jane, Samuel   Warren Twp.
     Admr - Jacob Bridges
     Admr de bonis non - Thomas Moore (B-296)

FLEMING, James             E-1851              pr 9-p 12, 15, 366
     Widow                                      B- 29, 30, 33
     children                                   Barlow
     Admr - David F. Fleming

FLEMING, Thomas L.         E-1840              pr 6-p 121, 122
     widow                                      pr 7-p 19
                                                Ludlow Twp.
     Admx - Priscilla Fleming

FLETCHER, Humphrey         E-1843              pr 5-p 148, 304
     widow & children got allowance but         pr 6-p 160
     not named                                  Adams Twp.
     Admr - Enoch Rector

FLINT, Eli                 W-1840              pr 6-p 39
     (of Greene Co., Penna.where will probated 1805)
     wife - Mary Flint
     son - William (under 16)
     dau - Minervy
     Admx - Mary Flint

FOGG, John Jacob           E-1849              pr 8-p 231, 253, 255, 459
     Admr - John Crawford                       Harmar-Marietta Twp.

FORD, Amon                 E-1845              pr 7-p 286, 287, 315
     widow - Hannah                             pr 8-p 36, 286
     children - Sarah S., Lucy A., Laura A.,    Watertown Twp.
               Jude & William Ford
     Admr - Ansel B. Ford

FORD, Giles                E-1797              pr 1-p 31, 32, 34
     Admr - William Ford                        Waterford Twp.
```

```
*FORD, Horatio N.              G-1831            pr 4-p 510
     son of William Ford, Jr.

     Guardian - Seth Hart


FORD, Horatio N.              W-1850            pr 8-p 402, 429
     wife - Lucy Ann Ford       (verbal)       pr 9-p 445
     legatee - Jas. Merrill if he stays with   Barlow Twp.
               Mrs. Ford until of age

     Admr - (C.T.A. or with will annexed) -
           wife - Lucy Ann Ford


*FORD, Isaiah N.              G-1831            pr 4-p 511
     son of William Ford, Jr.                  pr 5-p 105, 374
                                               Waterford Twp.
     Guardian - Giles H. Ford


FORD, Judah                   W-1851            pr 9-p 70, 89, 96
     sons - Chauncey D., Daniel                Watertown Twp.
     daus - Rosanna & Lucy E. Ford, single
            Caroline Ford Nellis, wife of O. Nellis
     grandsons - Hamilton Bishop, & Austin Bishop,
                 ch. of my eldest dau Harriet & Gilbert Bishop,
     grandson  - Misona Winslow Dunham, only ch of dau.
                 Louisa Ford Dunham

     Exrs - Ansel B. Ford, Chauncey D. Ford, Daniel Ford


*FORD, Lucian C.              G-1831            pr 4-p 510
       Romanta B.                              pr 5-p 376
     children of William Ford, Jr.             Watertown Twp.

     Guardian - Ansel B. Ford


FORD, William, Sr.            W-1823            pr 2-p 427
     wife - Artyonisa                          pr 3-p 83
     sons & daus - William, Jr., Judah, Chauncey,   pr 4-p 123
                   Truman, Lory Ford & Diana Woodford   Watertown Twp.
     grandson - Giles H. Ford

     Exr - Judah Ford


FORD, William, Jr.            W-1823            pr 2-p 245
     widow - Sarah                             pr 4-p119, 121, 344,510,511
     8 sons - Joseph N., Ansel B., & Amon R.   pr 6-p 68
              (of age); minors - Horatio N.,   Wooster Twp. (early name
              Lucian C., Romanta B., Isaiah N.,     for Watertown)
              & William P. Ford
     3 daus - Mary A. (mar. _____ Deming before
              settlement); Catherine P. (mar. ____
              Parke before settlement); & Julia A. Ford

     Exr - Joseph N. Ford
```

```
*FORD, William P.              G-1831          pr 4-p 511
    (son of William Ford, Jr.)                 pr 5-p 104, 376
                                               pr 6-p 69
    Guardian - Giles H. Ford                   Watertown Twp.


FORD, William P.               E-1839          pr 6-p 69
    dec'd minor son of William Ford, Jr., dec'd

    Guardian - Giles H. Ford


FORST, John                    W-1840          pr 6-p 43
    son - John M. Forst                        Roxbury Twp.
    daus - Tanezon, wife of Henry Gaddis (or Geddes);
        Rachel, wife of John H. Ralston; Mary,
        wife of John Morris
    children of dec'd son, Joseph Forst, namely -
        Susanah & Lewis Forst

    Exr - John M. Forst, son


FOSTER, Ephraim                E-1824          pr 2-p 501, 502
                                               pr 4-p 7
    Admr - Alexander Hill                      Fearing Twp.


FOSTER, Jane                   E-1831          pr 4-p 531
                                               pr 6-p 159
    Admr - William Burroughs                   Belpre Twp.


FOSTER, Leonard                E-1824          pr 3-p 95, 483
                                               Fearing Twp.
    Admx - Mrs. Ruth Ford


FOSTER, Milton                 W-1852          pr 9-p 100, 164, 463
                                               B-7
    wife - Jane                                Marietta
    ch - Hannah Sharlott Foster, John Milton Foster,
        Lewis Dexter Foster
    grandch - Rhoda Sophia McIntosh, Samuel Lewis McIntosh
            William Henry Wheeler, Mary Ann Foster

    Admr - Caleb Emerson; M. Clarke (1853)


FOSTER, Peregrine              W-1804          pr 1-p 63, 64
                                               pr 4-p 503
    wife - Mary                                Belpre Twp.
    bro - Dwight Foster, Esq.
    sons - Peregrine Pitt Foster, Frederick Augustus
        Foster & Theodore Sedgwick Foster
    daus - Polly Putnam, Seraph Dwight & Betsey
        Marietta Foster
    legatee - John Creed, 100 acres for faithful service

    Exr - William Rufus Putnam, of Marietta


FOWLER, John S.                E-1845          pr 7-p 313, 375
                                               Salem Twp.
    Admrs - Chester Tolman & John Perkins
```

```
FOX, William              W-1849              pr 8-p 343
    wife - Jane                               Independence Twp.
    sons - Patrick, William & James Fox
    daus - Sarah McVimic (or McVernic) & Mary McAnna


FRANKS, Henry             E-1845              pr 7-p 272, 339
    Admr - Owen Franks                        Grandview Twp.


FRAZER, James             E-1847              pr 8-p 82, 157
    Now in Ohio Penitentiary for life,        Warren Twp.
    estate for 4 minor children

    Admr - John Fulcher
    (note - James Frazer was not deceased)


FRAZER, John              E-1806              pr 1-p 61
                                              Marietta


FRAZIER, Christiana       W-1849              pr 8-p 251, 265, 272, 431
    (also other spellings)                    Barlow Twp.
    daus - Elizabeth Faris, Margaret Saunderson,
             and Christian Lamb
    son - James

    Exr - H. N. Ford who died in 1850; then
    Admr - William Lamb


FRAZIER, William          E-1837              pr 5-p 438, 440, 557
    widow and family                          Warren Twp.
    no names

    Admr - James Fraser (also sp. Frazer)


FRENCH, Isaac             W-1837              pr 5-p 386, 465
    wife - Electa                             pr 6-p 33
    6 daus - Eliza Buzzard, Melissa Dilly, Delila    Warren Twp.
             Postin, Electa I. Hopkins, Leta
             (or Lesa) French & Cintha French

    Execx - wife, Electa French


FRENCH, Nancy             W-1835              pr 5-p 253, 496
    son - Joseph French                       Union Twp.

    Exr - son, Joseph French


FRIEND, John              E-1800              pr 1-p 40
    of Massachusetts
    but died in Washington County, Ohio
    widow - Hannah Friend

    Admr - Ephraim Cutler, Esq.
```

FROTHINGHAM, Ebenezer, Jr.   W-1791   pr 1-p 7, 8
    wife - dec'd; children mentioned, not named   Marietta
    bros - Peter, John, Samuel
    sisters - Hannah & Lydia
    sisters-in-law - Betsey & Sally Boarman

    Exrs - Eben Frothingham (father) & Peter
           Frothingham (brother)

FROTHINGHAM, Peter   W-1798   pr 1-p 31
    ensign, late of the U.S. Army, dec'd

    will signed at Greenville
    bros - Samuel & John
    sisters - Hannah & Lydia

    Exrs - Samuel & Lydia

FRY, William   W-1821   pr 2-p 214, 230, 257
    (also FRYE)   pr 3-p 136
    wife - Phebe Fry, residing Shenandoah Co., Va.   Warren Twp.
    daus - Phebe, Leah, Rachel
    sons - Timothy & Gabriel

    Exr - Thos. Patten

FULCHER, Joseph   E-1836   pr 5-p 364
                                                pr 6-p 30
    Admr - John Fulcher   pr 7-p 184
                                                Warren Twp.

FULHAM, John   W-1797   pr 1-p 29, 48, 257
    (late of Ireland, of Rhode I. and of New
     Orleans in Spanish Dominion lying in
     Washington County, Northwest Territory)

    bro - Thomas Fulham, county of Eastmath, Ireland;
    other legatees - Peter Turner of E. Greenwich, R. I.;
                     Wanton Casey of Belpre

    Exrs - (named in will) Peter Turner & Wanton Casey;
           but, settlement signed by Isaac Pierce, Exr. in
           Washington Co.

FULLER, Solomon   W-1809   pr 1-p 171, 178
    wife - Ziperath Fuller   Marietta
    sons - Russel, Moses, Stephen (under 21) Samuel
    daus - Salley Porter, Lucy Sears; and (under 18)
           Almira, Lucretia & Betsey

    Exr - Moses Fuller

FULLER, Solomon   E-1845   pr 9-p 84, 87
    widow - Lucy   Marietta Twp.
    minor child

    Admr - William S. Fuller

*FULLER, Virgil   G-1848   pr 8-p 106
   lunatic
   has exhausted his part of his father, Charles
   Fuller's Estate (after his mother gets 1/3,
   there being 9 children, he is entitled to
   1/9 remainder) and Clerk should send certificate
   to Supt. of Ohio Lunatic Society notifying him

   Guardian - Robert T. Miller

FULLERTON, Daniel   E-1844   pr 7-p 98, 102
   widow   Warren Twp.
   one child

   Admr - William Fleming

FULLERTON, James   E-1824   pr 3-p 357
   widow - not named   Warren Twp

   Admr - (probably Wm Fleming who signed accounts)

*FULLERTON, William   G-1854   pr 9-p 515
   Guardian - Alexander McTaggart petitions to sell B-157, 158
               ward's land in Harmar, conveyed to him
               by John Crawford, admr of William Parker
               and is subject to dower of Elizabeth
               Fullerton, widow of Daniel Fullerton, dec'd

FULTON, James   E-1807   pr 1-p 130
                                                     Marietta

FULTON, Robert   Petition about   pr 9-p 574
        John   Salem Twp. road
BOYLES, John - petitioners   1854

FULTON, William   E-1824   pr 2-p 481, 482
   widow - Eliza Fulton   pr 3-p 316
   minor heirs -unnamed, with three gdns   pr 4-p 44
            James M. Booth, Joseph E. Hall,   Marietta
            Robert Williamson

   Admr - Lewis Anderson & admx, Eliza Fulton

GABAUDAN, John   E-1852   pr 9-p 172, 173
   widow - Eliza   Marietta Twp.

   Admr - Frederick A. Wheeler

GADDIS, Henry   E-1848   pr 8-p 157, 174, 175
   (also GEDDIS)   pr 9-p 412, 464, 517
   widow - Tamison (Tamzen)   B-131
   minor children - William & Edward
   ch. of full age - John F. Geddes of Franklin Co., Ohio;
                     Julia Ann Geddes, wife of John Geddes

   Admrs - John F. Gaddis of Franklin Co., Ohio & Isaac Baker

GAGE, Alpha S.   E-1851   pr 8-p 581, 582, 587
    widow - Nancy
    minor ch - Catharine A., Daniel A., Alpha W.

    Admr - Daniel Gage

GANNETT, Mary W.   W-1837   pr 5-p 335
    (wife of John M. Gannett of Hartford, Conn)
    where will proved 1825
    minor children - Samuel Wyllys Gannett, John Palgrave
                     Gannett, Catharine Mindell Gannett,
                     George Alfred Gannett, Caleb Thornton
                     Kirkland Gannett

    Exr - William Talcott

GANSEY, Joseph   W-1847   pr 7-p 588
    (age 72 at death, acc. to witnesses)   Wesley Twp.
    to wife, Mary, for life &
    at her death, residue to
    legatees - Thomas & Abraham Andrews
              (no relationship given)

    Execx - wife, Mary

GARD, John   E-1842
                      G-1842   pr 6-p 347
    (idiot)   Roxbury Twp.
    Guardian reports to be filed with
    estates of deceased persons

    Guardian - Samuel G. Williams

GARD, Nathan   E-1821   pr 2-p 245
                                         pr 3-p 305
    Admr - Michael Gard   Barlow Twp.

GARDNER, Amos   E-1813   pr 1-p 245
                                          Belpre Twp.
    Admx - Mary Gardner

GARDNER, John   E-1795   pr 1-p 14, 20, 22
                                          Gallipolis Twp.
    Admx - Margaret Little Gardner, widow

GARDNER, William C.   W-1846   pr 7-p 352
    (of Alexandria, D.C.
    where will proved, 1845)
    wife - Eliza Frances Gardner

    Execx - wife - Eliza

GATES, David   E-1828   pr 4-p 194, 224, 566
    widow - Pamela   Waterford Twp.

    Admx - Pamela Gates (signed by her mark)

GATES, Ebenezer   E-1848   pr 8-p 130, 133, 141,
                                                        374, 455
    widow - Mary Gates   pr 9-p 596
    7 children - one of whom was Arlee,   Marietta Twp.
    (pr 9-p 596) who mar. William W. Hart of
    Memphis, Tenn., and who died before 1855, leaving 3 minors;
    Mary F., Virginia W. & William W. Hart, Jr., whose gdn.,
    Samuel M. Gates was apptd. by Court, Shelby County, Tenn.

    Admrs - Mary Gates & William A. Whittlesey

GATES, John   E-1823   pr 2-p 322
    Admr - Samuel H. Gates   pr 3-p 262
                                        Marietta Twp.

GATES, Timothy   E-1822   pr 2-p 418, 419
                                        Waterford Twp.
    widow - Susanna Gates
    heirs - Jacob Gates; Timothy Gates, Jr.;   abbreviated as (Wf) below
             Timothy Gates, 2nd & wife, Susanna*;
             Samuel Loper and wife, Elizabeth (Betsey);
             Ruby Gates; Wilson L. Gates and wife,
             Mary*(Polly)

    No admr but agreement of heirs names
    3 appraisers to divide estate.
    *both Susanna & Mary had Gates as maiden name

    Washington County, Ohio Marriages:
    Gates, Timothy (Wf) to Hughs, Margaret (Wf) 14 May, 1800
        "   "   to Gates, Susanna*   25 Aug, 1807
        "   Wilson Lee to Gates, Mary*   7 Sept, 1815
    Loper, Samuel (wf) to Gates, Betsy (Wf)   4 June, 1816
    The starred * Susanna & Mary are probably children
    of Timothy Gates, the testator, and probably married
    cousins or other relatives

GATES, Timothy, 2nd   E-1833   pr 5-p 61, 62, 495
    widow - got allotment at appraisement but is not   Waterford Twp.
           named

    Admr - John Vincent

*GEAR, Jerusha   G-1847   pr 8-p 28
    Mary D.
    George R.
    Hiram L

    Guardian - Jerusha S. Gear

GERMAN, (Dr.) Morris   E-1834   pr 5-p 131, 482, 528
    widow - unnamed   Marietta
    child

    Admr - I. Humphreys

GEVREZ, Didier   E-1814   pr 1-p 269, 283, 315
    widow - also 2 children - got allowance but not   Marietta
        named
Admr - John B. Regnier

GIBBS, George   W-1837   pr 5-p 343
    (of Sunswick, in Newtown Twp., County of
    Queens, N.Y. State, but formerly of Newport,
    R. I.) Will proved in Queens, 1833)
    wife - Laura Gibbs
    children - no names
    Execx - wife, Laura

GIBSON, James   W-1819   pr 2-p 104, 138
    to Elizabeth Fleck, my mare (mother?)   Adams Twp.
    Charles Gibson - brother
    Exr - Charles Gibson

GIDDINGS, John   W-1826   pr 3-p 369, 535
                                                  pr 4-p 298
    widow - Hannah   Decatur Twp.
    sons - George, James, John
    daus - Aves Downing, Elizabeth, Ann & Maria
    grandson - John Giddings Downing
    Exr - James Giddings

GILBERT, Abel   E-1844   pr 7-p 81, 86
                                                  pr 8-p 143
    wife - Anna   B-151
    2 minor children - Rebecca & Abel, Jr.
    Admrs - Joel Gilbert & Caleb Engle

GILBERT, David   W-1839   pr 5-p 569
                                                  pr 6-p 61, 473, 474
    wife - Jemima   pr 7-p 21, 69
    dau - Charlotte   Marietta Twp.
    4 other children, not named
    Exr - R(obert) Crawford

GILLILAND, George S.   E-1852   pr 9-p 320, 321
    widow   B-52
    4 minor children under 15   Marietta Twp.
    Admr - Thomas W. Ewart

GILLINGHAM, Joseph   E-1840   pr 6-p 117
    widow and 7 children under age 15   Warren Twp.
    got an allowance - none named

*GILMORE, Sarah B.   G-1831   pr 4-p 544
        Isac M.
        David H.

        children of David Gilmore and heirs of
        Sarah Wiseman in her 1823 Will (pr 2-p 241)

    Guardian - John R. Gilmore

GLIDDEN, John   E-1818   pr 2-p 75, 97, 129
                                                       Fearing Twp.
    Admr - Elisha Allen

GLOVER, James   E-1825   pr 3-p 197
                                                       Marietta

GODDARD, Charles   E-1838   pr 5-p 515
                                                       Marietta Twp.
    All property for years' support of
    widow & children (not named)

GOLDSMITH, Benoni   W-1822   pr 2-p 234, 260, 399, 401
                                                       Fearing Twp.
    wife - Angelina
    sons - Burfit and John

    Exr - John Goldsmith

GOLDSMITH, John   E-1852   pr 9-p 249, 272
                                                       B-48, 50, 320
        ch - Mary Ann Wagg, Lydia Gibbon, James I.   Marietta
        Goldsmith, Susan Goldsmith, Lydia Ann
        Goldsmith, Nancy S. Unger (wife of
        Jonas Unger), Angeline Goldsmith
    Admr - Isaac N. Goldsmith

GOODALE, Nathan   E-1796   pr 1-p 19, 174, 184, 258
                                                       Belpre Twp.
        debts paid by Mrs. Elizabeth Goodale,
        relation not stated

    Admr - Isaac Pierce (Peirce)

GOODALE, Timothy   E-1796   pr 1-p 20, 270
                                                       Belpre Twp.
        (Timothy W.)

    Admr - Isaac Peirce

GOODMAN, Elizabeth   W-1846   pr 7-p 345, 379, 415
                                                       pr 8-p 347
        Children mentioned but unnamed in Will,   pr 9-p 225
        also, John Goodman, son of Mary Yeo, now   Fearing Twp.
        under age; called grandson in settlement,
        when Mary Yeo, Henry, William, Thomas & John
        Goodman all got equal payments as heirs,
        (children)

    Exr - John Collins

                                        Washington County, Ohio Probate -56-

GOODNO, Daniel   E-1833   pr 5-p 20, 23, 368
    widow - Sally Goodno   Belpre Twp.
    children

    Admr - D(aniel) H. Goodno

GORHAM, Benjamin E.   E-1845   pr 7-p 272, 275, 316
    widow & children   pr 8-p 111
    Admr - Richard D. Hollister   pr 9-p 591
                                                    B-237
                                                    Belpre Twp.

GOSS, Solomon   W-1828   pr 4-p 132
    sons - Solomon, Noah, Daniel, Levi   Fearing Twp.
    daus - Elizabeth Lake, Mary Goss
        and Lydia Goss

    Exr - Solomon Goss, son

GOSSETT, John, Jr.   E-1828   pr 4-p 246, 401, 424
    widow - Betsey Gossett   Barlow Twp.
    minor children - John Gossett, 3rd; Harriet, Giles,
                    Betsey, Mary Ann, Margaret; also
                    Matilda Miller, wife of Robert Miller

    Admr - Jabish F. Palmer

GOULD, Benjamin   W-1850   pr 8-p 403
    sons - Ephraim Gould, Daniel Gould   Salem Twp.
    daus - Mary A. Reyes, Philomena Gould,
        and Elizabeth Eastman
    grandson - Branerd Pago Gould
    other legatees - Mary, Melissa, Joseph D., Jasper P.
                    & Daniel W. Gould

    No exr named

GOULD, Daniel   E-1851   pr 9-p 82, 90, 91, 242
    widow - Jane   B-14
    minor ch. - Esther, Eliza, Luther   Salem Twp.
    other ch. - Mary, Jonas M., Julia L.

    Admr - Ephraim Gould

*GRAHAM, William   G-1853   pr 9-p 513
    insane   B-148

    Guardian - James Dunn

*GRAY, Elijah   G-1845   pr 7-p 186
    (minor heir of Samuel Gray, late of
    Belmont County, dec'd)

    Guardian - John Embree

*GRAY, Jesse   G-1845   pr 7-p 188
 (minor heir of Samuel Gray, late of
 Belmont County, dec'd)
 Accts. begin 1838
 Guardian - John Embree

*GRAY, Lemuel   G-1845   pr 7-p 187
 Accts. begin 11-6-1841
 Guardian - John Embree

GRAY, Matthew   E- 1841   pr 6-p 181, 355
 widow & 1 child under 15 got support   pr 7-p 48
                 pr 8-p 292
 Admr - Wm Crawford   Liberty Twp.
 Admr de bonis non - Wm T. Bascom (from Sept., 1844)

*GRAY, Samuel   G-1845   pr 7-p 188
 (minor heir of Samuel Gray, late of
 Belmont County, dec'd)
 Accts. begin, 1838
 Guardian - John Embree

GRAY, William   E-1812   pr 1-p 209, 246
 Admx - Mary Gray; Eli G. Cogswell, asst.   Waterford Twp.

GREEN, Duty   W-1842   pr 6-p 379, 432
 daus - Margaret Woodruff & Pamelia Renolds pr 8-p 145
 sons - Duty, Caleb, Smith & Eli Green   Barlow Twp.
 Exr - Caleb Green, son

GREEN, Ezra   W-1822   pr 2-p 271, 375
 wife - Anna (Anne)   Adams Twp.
 son - Stephen Washington Green (minor)
 daus - Sally M. & Elizabeth Green
 bro - Willard M. Green
 Exrs - John Green, Esq. of Adams Twp. &
    John Brown, Esq. of Ames Twp., Athens Co., Ohio

GREEN, Henry F.   pr 7-p 582
  and Caroline F. Green
vs Atkinson Heirs
 Notice of petition for partition - 1843
 Petition to divide real estate notifying five
 Atkinsons - Eliza S., Emma F., Angeline & James
 also, Emma L. & Alexander Fleming. Land is in Decatur Twp. -
  262 acres, lot #33, Sec. 27, Town 6, Range 11 in Washington
  County; also some in Gallia County

GREEN, John   W-1833   pr 5-p 1, 2, 58, 506
    present wife - Eliza Green   Marietta, formerly
    1st wife - T. P. Green   of Adams Twp.
    son - John Green, 2nd
    dau - Phebe G. Ross

    Execx - Eliza Green

GREEN, Nancy   E-1824   pr 3-p 89
                                               Adams Twp.

GREEN, Sally M.   E-1833   pr 5-p 60, 239
    Admr - John Hougland   Barlow Twp.

GREEN, Sarah   E-1840   pr 6-p 81, 123, 129, 344
    (GREENE, Sally)   G-1840   pr 7-p 479

    Admr - A. T. Nye, was also guardian for Sarah (insane)

GREENE, Griffin   E-1804   pr 1-p 66, 91, 96, 103
    widow - Sarah Greene   Marietta

    Admr - Philip Greene

GREENE, Griffin   W-1852   pr 9-p 98, 341, 343, 356
    legacies to Sally Green of Harmar, William B-3
    Greeneof Putnam, Robert R. Greene of Illinois,   Marietta
    Richard Greene of Harmar, Caroline Hutchinson
    of Warren, relation not stated

    Admr - William Devol

GREENE, James H.   W-1843   pr 6-p 463
    to father, Daniel Greene with whom he was Marietta
    partner in firm, D. Greene & Son

    Exr - Daniel Greene

GREENE, John   E-1813   pr 1-p 243, 244, 274, 281
    Admr - Daniel Greene   Newport Twp.

GREENE, Mary   W-1823   pr 2-p 434
    (widow of John Greene, Sr.)   pr 3-p 91, 93, 198
    daus - Eliza, Ruth, Mary   Newport Twp.
    granddaus - Eliza W. Haskell, Maria Haskell
    sons - Daniel & John

    Exr - John Greene, Jr.

GREENE, Philip   E-1807   pr 1-p 97, 103, 104
    Admr - Griffin Greene, Jr.   Marietta

```
GREENE, Philip                    E-1842              pr 6-p 285
    Admr - Richard Greene                             Newport Twp.

GREENE, Richard                   E-1805              pr 1-p 77
                                                      Marietta

GREENE, Richard S.                E-1839              pr 6-p 35
                                                      Marietta

GREENE, Sarah                     W-1813              pr 1-p 232
    (widow of Griffin Greene, Sr.)                    Marietta
    son - Griffin Greene
    granddaus - Caroline & Sarah Greene
    grandsons (under 21) - William R., Robert R.
                    and Richard Greene
    also, legacies to friend, Barshabe  Greene and to
        Lydia Ackley & mention of dec'd dau, Susan
        Camock, dec'd, son-in-law, John Camock, and
        dec'd son, Phillip

    Exr - Griffin Greene (son)

GREENE, Willard                   E-1839              pr 5-p 597
                                                      pr 6-p 254
    widow - Elizabeth Greene                          Warren Twp.
        (Greene also spelled Green)

    Admx - Elizabeth Greene

GREENLEES, Archibald              E-1826              pr 3-p 447, 533
                                                      pr 4-p 99, 335
    widow - Mary (mar. 2nd Samuel Patton of           Belpre Twp.
        Fearing, 15 Dec., 1826)
    no children - only heir, bro. William Greenlees,
        resident of Argyleshire, North Britain

    Admr - James Harvey, Jr.

GREENLEES, John                   E-1848              pr 8-p 127, 128, 140, 287
                                                      Barlow Twp.
    widow

    Admr - Jacob Bridges

*GREENLEES, John Jr.              G-1852              pr 9-p 196
    son of John Greenlees dec'd
    payments to Elizabeth Greenlees (probably his mother)

    Guardian - William Fullerton

GREENMAN, Jeremiah                W-1829              pr 4-p 260
    wife - Mary Greenman                              Waterford Twp
    sons - John Greenman, Esek Eddy Greenman,
            Jeremiah Greenman
    dau - Mary Dunham

    Execx - wife, Mary Greenman
```

GRIDLEY, William   W-1837   pr 5-p 419
    (of Boston, Mass. where will
    probated, 1836)

    son - William Gridley
    dau - (?)-Betsey Perry, wife of Joseph Perry of New Haven, Conn.
    dau - Marietta Capen, wife of Josiah Capen of Boston

    Exr - son, William Gridley

GRIFFITH, Emlin   E-1840   pr 6-p 143, 146
    widow   pr 8-p 23
    children   Wesley Twp.

    Admrs - Thomas Penrose & Samuel W. Smith

GRIMES, Benjamin   E-1848   pr 8-p 159, 160, 175
    widow and 1 minor child under age 15,   Roxbury Twp.
          received year's allowance

    Admr - Noah Bailey

GROVES, William   E-1841   pr 6-p 203, 209
    widow & heirs got support for 1 yr.   Roxbury Twp.

    Admr - Hiram Gard

GRUBB, Peter   E-1829   pr 4-p 257
    Admx - Elizabeth Grubb   Waterford Twp.

GRUBB, William   E-1791   pr 1-p 5
    (Soldier in service of U.S.)

    Admr - Capt. David Zeigler

GUILINGER, Martin   W-1852   pr 9-p 97, 103
                                    B-1, 95
    wife - Eve   Newport Twp.
    sons - Michael, Jacob, Thomas
        John, James, Seth, Joseph
    dau - Catharine

    Admr - Michael Guilinger

GUITTEAU, Adoniram J.   E-1823   pr 2-p 550, 552
    widow - Sarah Guitteau (mar. Dr. Ephraim   pr 4-p 93, 200
       Quinby of Fearing, 12 July, 1825)   Fearing Twp.
    children - all minors - Maria, Eliza Ann, Adoniram J.,
        Patience Guitteau

    Admx - Sarah Guitteau, later Sarah Quinby

GUITTEAU, Benjamin   E-1831   pr 4-p 492
    widow - Maria   pr 5-p 82, 102
    ch of full age - William H. & Francis   Fearing Twp.
        Guitteau; Jane Williams, wife of
        Thomas Williams
    minor children - Eliza Ann, Caroline, Emeline,
        Benjamin & John Guitteau

    Admr - William H. Guitteau (son)

GUITTEAU, Edward   E-1823   pr 2-p 546
    Heirs - Wm. R. Putnam & Jerusha, his wife;   pr 3-p 306 (petition)
        Jonas Moore & Patience, his wife;   pr 4-p 267, 274
        Benjamin, Minerva & Ann Idia Guitteau   Marietta
        of full age; also heirs of Jonathan
        Guitteau & of Adoniram J. Guitteau, dec'd
    Heirs of Jonathan Guitteau, dec'd were
        minors - Abner Lord Guitteau, Julia and
        Sarah Guitteau
    Heirs of Adoniram J. Guitteau, dec'd were -
        minors - Maria, Eliza Ann & Judson Guitteau

    Admr - William R. Putnam

GUITTEAU, Jonathan   E-1822   pr 2-p 354
    Admr - William R. Putnam   pr 5-p 97, 99, 152
                                               Marietta

GUITTEAU, Judson   E-1823   pr 2-p 548
    Admr - Wm. R. Putnam   pr 4-p 269, 275
                                               Marietta

GUITTEAU, Minervy   W-1851   pr 8-p 591
    bequests to relations,   pr 9-p 106, 196
    Abner L. Guitteau and his sister Sarah Guitteau   Marietta

    Exr - Abner L. Guitteau

GUITTEAU, William H.   E-1848   pr 8-p 114, 116, 139, 225
    widow   Fearing Twp.
    children

    Admr - Josiah Morgan

GUTHRIE, Stephen   E-1827   pr 4-p 133, 135, 332, 384
    widow - not named, got an allowance   Belpre Twp.
    Heirs - A. A. Guthrie, Stephen H. Guthrie,
        E. Guthrie, Walter Curtis & A. Dunham

    Admrs - Erastus Guthrie & Walter Curtis

GUTHRIE, Truman   W-1841   pr 6-p 151, 471
    7 sons - Edwin, Truman, Jr., Augustus S.,   Belpre Twp.
        James H., Charles L., Benjamin F.,
        and David Q. Guthrie

    Admr - Edwin Guthrie (son)

GUYTON, Thomas M.   E-1852   pr 9-p 240, 241
    Admr - Enoch Dye   B-37
                                           Lawrence Twp.

HAAS, George   W-1853   pr 9-p 359, 461
    friend - Jacob Avineshand (Owenshane) B-72
                                           Union Twp.
    Exr - Jacob Avineshand

HAGERMAN, James   E-1842   pr 6-p 419, 421
    Admrs - Peter Hagerman & John Callahan pr 8-p 186
                                           Waterford Twp.

HAGERMAN, Peter   W-1849   pr 8-p 252, 258, 259,
    wife - Betsey   270, 565
    heirs of dau. Hannah (viz John Hagerman) Watertown Twp.
    Heirs of dau Betsey
    daus - Mariah Callahan, Lettica Hamilton & Rebecca Morey
    sons - James, Bailey; also, Aaron & John

    Exrs - Cyrus Morey & Samuel Wood

HAIGHT, Gilbert   E-1846   pr 7-p 371, 394, 429
    widow - Mercy Haight   pr 8-p 187
    children - (unnamed)   Newport Twp.

    Admx - Mercy Haight (widow)

HALE, Christian   W-1837   pr 5-p 425, 466, 470
    "friend" - Margaret Jackson, maybe wife pr 6-p 157
    George Hale - relation not stated   Salem Twp.
    4 children - Jacob Hale, Michael Hale, Andrew Hale,
                and Catherine ?Macek?

    Exr - Joseph Reed

    Note- the will speaks of "my friend - Margaret Jackson" who
    must be his wife, as there is a marriage in Washington Co.,
    Ohio of Hale, Christian to Jackson, Margaret on 24 March, 1809,
    both of Salem
    Also, at the sale of personal property, there are articles to
    Mrs. Hale

HALL, James   E-1824   pr 3-p 237, 272
    Admr - Caius M. Wood   pr 4-p 39
                                           Union Twp.

HALLEY, William   W-1808   pr 1-p 155, 156, 160
    (formerly of Alexandria, D.C. where will Marietta
    signed 1805, with codicil in Marietta, 1808)
    wife - Esther Halley (also called Mehitable)
    5 other heirs (unnamed), each to get 1/6
    after special provision for wife

    Exrs - (named in will) - Esther Halley (wife) & Coleman Brown
            of Fairfax Co., Va. & Edward Stabler, of town of
            Alexandria

HAMILTON, Samuel W.   E-1841   pr 6-p 239, 241
    widow & 8 children got year's support   Lawrence Twp.

    Admx - Eliza Hamilton

HAMMON, Zoeth   E-1802   pr 1-p 51, 55, 65, 149
    Heirs - Anna Seamons, Allison Hammond, Moriby (?) Waterford Twp.
       Forest, Benjamin Hammond, & Hannah McBride
    Note - I should have listed above that
    HAMMON IS ALSO SP. HAMMOND

    Admr - Wanton Devoll

HANDLIN, Patrick   E-1826   pr 3-p 535
    widow - all property for her support   Ludlow Twp.

    Appraisers only - no admr.

HARMON, John   E-1800   pr 1-p 37
    Admr - Nehemiah Sprague   Waterford Twp.

HARPER, Thomas   E-1818   pr 2-p 114
    Appraisement only   Marietta
    No admr.

HARRIS, Willard   E-1851   pr 9-p 75,77
    widow   Warren Twp.

    Admr - Jacob Bridges

*HART, Elizabeth   G-1829   pr 4-p 251
      Hawkins   Waterford Twp.
      Josiah

    (All are heirs of Josiah Hart, dec'd)
    In gdn. accts. Elizabeth was described as the late
    Elizabeth Hart, but she may be married rather than dead

    Guardian - Simeon Deming

*HART, Henry W.   G-1845   pr 7-p 161
    (one of minor heirs of R. G. Hart, late of   pr 8-p 197, 199, 597
    Memphis, Tenn.)

    Guardian - Seth Hart

HART, Josiah   E-1808   pr 1-p 114
                                   pr 3-p 168, 169(partition)
    Left 3 minor heirs, but by the time of   pr 4-p 251 (gdn. accts.)
    1824 petition for partition, Betsey Hart had   Waterford Twp.
    married Nathan Wheeler
    Other heirs were - Hawkins Hart, Josiah Hart, Jr.

    Guardian - Simeon Deming

*HART, Josiah T.   G-1845   pr 7-p 159
    (one of minor heirs of Royal G. Hart,   pr 8-p 197, 198
    late of Memphis, Tenn.)
    This & other settlements for children sworn to
    by guardian & certified also by May Hart, probably
    their mother

    Guardian - Seth Hart

*HART, Mary F.   G-1855   pr 9-p 596
    Virginia W.   B-261
    William W., Jr.
    minor ch. of William W. and Arlee Hart of
    Memphis, Tenn., whose guardian appt. by Court in
    Shelby Co., Tenn petitions to sell land left by their
    grandfather, Ebenezer Gates in Washington County, Ohio

    Guardian - Samuel M. Gates

*HART, Matilda Ann   G-1845   pr 7-p 158
    (one of minor heirs of R. G. Hart,   pr 8-p 197, 200, 594
    late of Memphis, Tenn.)

    Guardian - Seth Hart

*HART, May Jonathan   G-1845   pr 7-p 157
    (one of minor heirs of R. G. Hart,
    late of Memphis, Tenn.)

    Guardian - Seth Hart

HARVEY, John   W-1850   pr 8-p 451, 523, 533, 535
                                                       pr 9-p 115, 211
    7 sisters - Ann Greenlees, Martha Breakenridge,   Barlow Twp.
                Jane Harvey, Margaret Breakenridge,
                Martha Harvey, Mary Harvey,
                Nancy Harvey

    1 bro - James Harvey
    heirs of Catherine McCuig, dec'd
    heirs of Samuel Harvey, dec'd

    Exr - friend, John Breckenridge of Roxbury

HARVEY, Mary   E-1852   pr 9-p 251, 270
                                                       B-41
    Admr - Robert Greenlees   Barlow Twp

HARVEY, Samuel   E-1841   pr 6-p 230, 233, 444
                                                       pr 8-p 602
    widow - Isabella mar. 2nd - D. N. Dunsmoor   Barlow Twp.
    child - Samuel W. Harvey, only heir

    Admr - James Harvey

*HARVEY, Samuel W.   G-1849   pr 8-p 307
    son of Samuel Harvey   pr 9-p 62
                                                       B-258
    1st Guardian - James Harvey
    Guardian at settlement - David F. Fleming

```
HARVIE, James              W-1847        pr 8-p 7, 118, 140, 346
  (Harvey)                               Warren Twp.
  son - James, Jr. (unmarried)
  daus - Catharine, Jean, Mary, Anne (unmarried)
       Margaret, Jackey (unmarried), also
       Martha & Agnes

  Exr - James Harvie, Jr.


HARWARD, Henry             E-1845        pr 7-p 232, 321
                                         Adams Twp.
  widow and 2 children - unnamed

  Admr - Charles Harward


HASKELL, Charles           E-1831        pr 4-p 549
                                         pr 5-p 271
  widow & 2 children                     Newport Two.

  Admr - Charles Dana


HASKELL, Jonathan          W-1816        pr 1-p 317
                                         Belpre Twp.
  only heirs - 4 children
  sons - Charles and John Greene Haskell
  daus - Maria and Eliza Haskell

  Exrs - Aaron Waldo Putnam & Cyrus Ames


HASKELL, Moses             E-1819        pr 2-p 143, 145, 183,
                                                   184, 206
  Admr - John Gates                      Marietta


HATCH, James               W-1840        pr 6-p 92, 117(will),
  (of Olive Twp., Morgan Co., when will written,      123, 345
  1830, but came later to Marietta Twp.)  Marietta Twp.

  dau - Sally
  grandchildren - Barzilla, Uriah, Lydia Haskell
                  and Harriet Pinkham

  Admr - Daniel F. Harper (after named exr refused)


HAYWARD, Edward N.         E-1850        pr 8-p 430, 545
                                         pr 9-p 111
  Admr - George B. Hayward               Waterford Twp.


HAYWARD, George            W-1852        pr 9-p 161, 201, 203, 297
                           verbal        B-28, 156
  wife - Henrietta                       Waterford Twp.
  minor son - George W.

  Admr - George Vincent


HAYWARD, Rotheus           W-1842        pr 6-p 313, 332
                                         pr 7-p 53, 480
  wife - (not named)                     pr 9-p 437
  sons - Rotheus & Edward N. Hayward     Waterford Twp.
  daus - Minerva Shaw, also Charlotte C. & Panthe
         N. Hayward

  Exrs - Anselm T. Nye & B. T. Hayward
```

HAZARD, Ebenezer   W-1839   pr 5-p 567

    wife - Abigail
    children - Samuel, Elizabeth & Erskine Hazard

    Exrs - wife, Abigail & sons, Samuel and Erskine
    note - omitted above - (Ebenezer Hazard, testator was
        from Philadelphia Co., Pa. but no date of
        probate given)

HEALD, Levi   W-1853   pr 9-p 377, 450, 465
    wife - Lydia   B-76
    son - Samuel is surviving partner   Wesley Twp.
    minor ch. - Mary Ann

    Exrs - wife, Lydia & son, Samuel

HEALD, Smith   W-1853   pr 9-p 378, 452, 465
    wife - Achsah   B-76, 113, 114, 122
    children - not named in will, but 3 minors   Wesley Twp.
          got year's support - Maryetta,
          Milton, Ruthann

    Execx - wife, Achsah

HEARN, Josiah G. K.   E-1847   pr 7-p 617
    wife - Rachel   pr 8-p 42, 421
    minor children - Wingett, Daniel, Henry,   Ludlow Twp.
          Horace & Josiah Hearn

    Admr - Jacob Winget

HEART, Alies Evelyne   W-1837   pr 5-p 383
    (of Hartford, Conn. where will
    probated, 1805)

    wife - Charlotte Heart, but no children
    mother - Mrs. Abigail Strong (wife of Rev.
        Cyprian Strong of Chatam) also
    father-in-law - Seth Overton, of Chatam

    Exr - Seth Overton

HEART, Jonathan   W-1817   pr 2-p 30
    heir - William Heart, son of Dr. Josiah
        Heart of Weathersfield, Conn.

HELLET, Isaiah   W-1824   pr 3-p 122
    wife - Anna   Salem Twp.

    Execx - wife, Anna

HEMPSTEAD, Giles   E-1826   pr 3-p 377, 445, 453, 493
    heirs - G.S.B. Hempstead, Lucretia Hempstead,   pr 5-p 560
        and Harriet Hempstead   Marietta

    Admr - G.S.B. Hempstead

```
*HENDERSHOT, Francis M.        G-1854              pr 9-p 555
              Louisa                               B-181, 184
              Lucinda
              Jonathan Jr.
              Chauncey
              Perry M.
         6 heirs of their mother, Elizabeth recently dec'd
         petition to sell lands in Liberty Twp.

         Guardian & father - Jonathan Hendershot

HENDERSON, Adam               E-1851              pr 9-p 9, 24, 370
                                                  B-15, 27, 263
         widow - Isabella                         Ludlow Twp.
         ch under 15 - Eliza Jane, Daniel, John F.,
                       Robert D. & Joseph C. W. Henderson

         Admr - Alexander Bell

HENDERSON, Edward             E-1801              pr 1-p 48, 68, 200
         Admx - Sally Henderson, later Sally Ward  pr 2-p 7, 8, 9
                                                  Belpre Twp.

HENRY, John                   E-1852              pr 9-p 139, 141, 408, 464
         5 heirs rec'd equal amts - John B., Nathan P. and  B-8, 52, 92
                   Phebe J. Henry; Julian A. Henry by his   Barlow Twp.
                   guardian, Caleb Green, William R. Henry

         Admr - William R. Henry

HENRY, Robert                 W-1845              pr 7-p 146, 172, 174, 586
                                                  Watertown Twp.
         wife - Roxanna
         6 sons - Joel, Joseph, John, Daniel W.,
                  Benjamin Franklin & George Owen Henry
         6 daus - Prussia Ann, Mary, Martha, Elizabeth,
                  Harriet E., & Lucy Henry

         Exr - Charles G. Culver

HENRY, Robert, 2nd            W-1840              pr 6-p 83, 120
                                                  pr 7-p 47
         wife - Elizabeth                         Watertown Twp.
         sons - John & David
         daus - Hannah, Betsey & Mary

         Exr - David Henry, youngest son

HENSEL, John                  W-1848              pr 8-p 177
         wife - Margaret
         sons - John, Samuel & Nathaniel
         daus - Katherine Haught, Ann Mary Whitney,
                Sarah Whitney & Marget Highley

         Exr - not named in will

HENTON, John                  E-1847              pr 8-p 84, 85, 101, 280
         Admr - William Caywood, Jr.              Fearing Twp.
```

HERSEY, Isaac B.   E-1818
    Heirs - Achsah Hersey & Betsey Hersey
        both of Windsor Twp., Morgan Co.,
        Ohio at time of settlement, in 1821
    Admr - Franklin Hersey

pr 2-p 115, 181, 217
Roxbury Twp.

HERSEY, Martin   E-1802
    widow - Mary (or Mercy) who married
        2nd Asa Cheadle, Jr. (1-20-1802)
    Admx - widow, Mary Hersey
    Admr - Asa Cheadle, Jr.

pr 1-p 48, 49, 50, 90
Adams Twp.

HIETT, John   E-1823
    Admr. - David Gard

pr 2-p 513
pr 3-p 286
Barlow Twp. (1st ref.)
Wesley Twp. (2nd ref.)

HIETT, Timothy   E-1839
    widow - unnamed
    children & heirs - wife of Evan Jenkins;
        wife of George Uhl; wife of David Gard;
        Ruth Hiett; James Hiett, Samuel Hiett;
        heirs of John Hiett (namely, Austin
        Hiett, George C. Hiett, the wife of
        Daniel Tilton & S. D. Hiett)
    Admr - Joseph Palmer

pr 6-p 27, 201
pr 9-p 113
Roxbury Twp.

HILDEBRAND, George   E-1827
    widow - Elizabeth
    2 children in Wash. Co - John Hildebrand of
        Wesley Twp. & Polly Vial, wife of Daniel
        Vial of Watertown Twp.; also Susanna
        Depros, wife of Peter Depros of Missouri;
        George Hildebrand of Freeport, Pa.
    additional heirs: Betsey Little of Jefferson Co., Ohio;
        Nancy Booker, wife of George Booker of Canton,
        Stark Co., Ohio; also 3 heirs of Pittsburgh, Pa.:
        Solomon Hildebrand, Sarah Wood, Joel Hildebrand

                9 children
    Admr - Jesse Hildebrand

pr 4-p 137, 139, 302
pr 5-p 29
Fearing Twp.

HILL, Alexander   E-1841
    widow
    Admr - Hugh Hill, 2nd

pr 6-p 161
pr 8-p 107
Marietta

HILL, Alexander   E-1845
    at settlement in 1850,
    Alexander Hill, Jr. is only surviving admr.
    Admrs - Alexander Hill, Jr. &
          William M. (or H.) Hill

pr 7-p 164, 166, 317
pr 8-p 420
Watertown Twp.

HILL, Atkinson   E-1845   pr 7-p 231
    widow & children mentioned, but no names   Beverly in Waterford Twp.
    Admr. - Stephen Hill

HILL, Elizabeth   E-1851   pr 8-p 615
    Admr - Benjamin F. Gilpin

HILL, Ira   W-1842   pr 6-p 313
    wife - Esther Hill   Salem Twp.
    children - Ira, Harry & Sally Hill;
        also, Urania Stanley and
        sons - Guy Hill & Dan Hill

    Exr - Guy Hill served; Dan also named in will

HILL, Matthew   W-1849   pr 8-p 248
    wife - Mary
    son - David C. Hill

    No exr named in will

HILL, Richard   E-1820   pr 2-p 194
    Heirs received property before father's   Fearing Twp.
    death, namely: Polly Baldin, Martha Kidd,
    Ruth Chapman, Jane Mitchell & James Hill

HILL, Stephen   E-1847   pr 7-p 619, 621
                                                           pr 8-p 41
    Admr - Samuel B. Robinson   pr 9-p 57
                                                           Waterford Twp.

HILL, William   E- 1821   pr 2-p 239, 240, 280, 511
    Exr - James Williamson   Grandview Twp.

HILL, William   W-1830   pr 4-p 353, 409, 412, 589
    wife - Sarah   Lawrence Twp.
    sons - John & William
    daus - Maria; Mary Greene; Elizabeth Taylor,
        wife of Jasher Taylor; Margaret McVay,
        wife of Reuben McVay

    Exrs - sons, John & William Hill, Jr.

HINKLEY, Nathaniel   E-1840   pr 6-p 148
    widow   Watertown Twp.

    Admr - Hiram Gard

*HOFF, Eleanor   G-1831   pr 4-p 506
    (formerly Eleanor Chambers
    dau. of John Chambers)
    settlement

    Guardian - William Nixon

HOFF, John F.   E-1812   pr 1-p 235, 236, 286
    widow - Elizabeth Hoff   Fearing Twp.

    Admr - Simeon Tuttle

HOLDEN, William   E-1848   pr 8-p 120
    Admr - Rufus E. Harte   Marietta

HOLDREN, Joseph   E- 1824   pr 3-p 231, 444
    widow - Ruth and family, yr's allowance Grandview Twp.
    heirs - Samuel Holdren and
            Grace Parr, named later

    Admrs - Coleman Holdren & Ruth Holdren

HOLT, John   E-1807   pr 1-p 117, 118, 119, 198
    Admr - Richard Holt   Marietta

HOOK, Henry K.   E-1837   pr 5-p 437
    Partnership with William Knox in   pr 6-p 13
    Boatyard of Hook & Knox, and as   Marietta Twp.
    owner of boat "S. B. Tuscumbria"

    Admrs - William Knox & Mary Hook

HORTON, Amos   W-1840   pr 6-p 37
    (of Mason, Providence Plantations, R.I.
     where will probated 1811)

    wife - Chloe Horton
    dau - Mary Walker & her children
    son - Andrew
    "All my children & Betsey Streeter, dau
     of son Samuel"

    Exr - wife & friend, John Holden

HOUGHTON, Thomas   E-1847   pr 7-p 579
    (late of Columbiana Co., Ohio, but
     died at St. Louis, Mo.)
    Appraisal of personal property
    in Washington County taken here)

HOUGLAND, Mrs. Anna   E-1824   pr 3-p 164, 345
    Admr - B. F. Palmer   Barlow Twp.

HOUGLAND, Cornelius   E-1818   pr 2-p 78, 81, 93, 135, 167
    Admr - Jabish F. Palmer   Wesley Twp.; also
    Admx - Anna Hougland, widow   Barlow Twp. given

```
*HOUGLAND, Lewis              G-1827          pr 4-p 87, 459
    minor and heir-at-law of Cornelius
    Hougland, late of Barlow, dec'd
    1st Guardian - John Hougland
    2nd Guardian - Gilbert Bishop, Jr.
    3rd Guardian - Joseph Palmer

HOVEY, John                   E-1851          pr 9-p 4, 396
    widow                                     B-192, 222
    3 minor ch - Milton, George, Abbey D.     Marietta

    Admrs - James B. Hovey, John D. Hovey

HOWARD, Edward W.             W-1804          pr 1-p 60, 61
    Legatees - Bridget Force of Marietta Twp.;    Marietta
        Edward Howard, son of Henry Howard;
        son, Henry Howard

    Exrs - John Brough, Esq. & Bridget Force

HOWE, Aaron                   W-1812          pr 1-p 202, 210
    wife - Rachel                             Marietta
    sons - George & Chester

    Exr - George Howe

HOWE, George                  W-1823          pr 2-p 438
    wife - Mary                               pr 3-p 105, 108
    mother - Rachel Howe                      Marietta

    Exr - George Corner & wife, Mary Howe

HOWE, Hiram                   E- 1843         pr 6-p 481
    Admr - Solomon Fuller                     pr 7-p 585
                                              Marietta Twp.

HOWE, Rufus W.            Hab. Corp.-1855     pr 9-p 613

HOWISON, Robert               E-1844          pr 7-p 126
    widow - E. H. Howison                     pr 8-p 464

    Admr - John C. McCoy

HUBBARD, Roswell              E-1845          pr 7-p 196, 197
    Admr - Butler Wells                       pr 8-p 29
                                              Grandview Twp.

HUGGINS, Benjamin             W-1847          pr 7-p 472
    wife - Elizabeth B. Huggins               pr 9-p 1, 2, 365, 462
    6 sons - David, Enoch, John, Jason,       B-132
        George William & Justin               Union Twp., later
    2 daus - Phebe Mary & Beulah              Warren Twp.

    Execx - wife & Exr John Crawford of Harmar
    2nd, Admr de bonis non - John Huggins
```

HUGHES, William S.   E-1809   pr 1-p 174, 175, 178
    Admr - Isaac Mixer, Jr.   Marietta

HUMMEL, Jacob   E-1802   pr 1-p 48, 52
    Admr - Thomas Hummel   Newton, a twp. now in
                                            Muskingum Co., Ohio

HUMPHREY, Elisha   W-1845   pr 7-p 254, 282, 314, 580
    wife - Hannah   pr 8-p 188
    2 orphans - Elizabeth & Hart Bloomfiel Watertown Twp.
    nephews - Joseph S., James W., Cromwell C.,
        Julius, Mark & Stephen Humphrey
    nephew of former wife - Elisha Dowling
    niece - Eliza H. Alderman
    sister - Mary Oviatt
    nephew - Cyrus Elisha Oviatt
    niece - Amanda E. Oviatt

    Exrs - Joseph S. Humphrey & Robert B. Parke

HUMPHREY, Seth   E-1827   pr 4-p 143, 145, 246,
                                                    309, 376
    widow - Olive   Watertown Twp.
    ch of full age - Joseph S. Humphrey
    minors - James W., Eliza H., Elizabeth P.
        & Elijah C. Humphrey

    Admr - Joseph S. Humphrey

HUMPHREYS, Charles   E-1846   pr 7-p 309
    Admr - Isaac Humphreys

HUMPHREYS, Isaac   W-1850   pr 8-p 447, 479, 482, 523
    son - Joseph Bloomfield Humphreys   pr 9-p 318
    dau - Elizabeth, wife of Caleb Bates   Harmar
        of Cincinnati
    dau - Mary Ann Deming, wife of Joel Deming
    son - Henry Nelson Humphreys
    dec'd dau - Harriet, late wife of Stephen Newton
    6 other legatees

    Exr - Douglas Putnam

HUNT, Joseph   W-1830   pr 4-p 356
    dau - Hannah Hall   Salem Twp.
    son-in-law - Aaron Hall
    grandson - Joseph Hunt Hall
    dau - in Pa. - Phebe Matson
    grandaus - Elizabeth Hunt Hall & Mary Hall

    Exrs - Simon Porter & John True

*HURLBUT, Lydia   G-1795   pr 1-p 16
    orphan & minor

    Guardian - Thomas Stanley of Marietta

HUTCHINS, Shubel   E-1833   pr 5-p 94, 96, 527
   widow & 3 children   Aurelius Twp.

   Admr - Joseph Davis
   Admx - Rhoda Hutchins

HUTCHINSON, Augustus J.   E-1828   pr 4-p 193, 333
   Admr - Benj. F. Palmer   Barlow Twp.

HUTCHINSON, John   E-1845   pr 7-p 316
   Admr - Joseph Palmer   Barlow Twp.

HUTCHINSON, John F.   G-1846   pr 7-p 390
                     E-1846   pr 8-p 33

   (Believe this deceased minor was son of
   Augustus J. & Eleanor (Gard) Hutchinson.
   She married 2nd Thomas Rodgers of Watertown,
   17 June, 1830)

   Guardian - Thomas & Eleanor Rodgers
   Admr - Joseph Palmer

*HUTCHINSON, Julia et al   G-1851   pr 8-p 599

   (Dudley, John T.)
   minor ch. of Thomas Hutchinson

   Guardian - Wm W. Hutchinson

HUTCHINSON, Thomas   E-1805   pr 1-p 153, 189
   (Hutchison)   Marietta

   Admr - Ichabod Nye

HUTCHINSON, Thomas   E-1842   pr 6-p 363
   widow & 3 children got yr's support;   pr 8-p 587, 599
   gdn. accts. give children's names as:
   Julia, Dudley & John T. Hutchinson, with
   gdn. Wm W. Hutchinson (1851)

   Admrs - William Warren, Nancy Hutchinson

HUTSON, John   E-1839   pr 5-p 573
   Admr - J. P. Wightman   pr 6-p 314
                              Marietta Twp.

*HUYSINGTON, George   G-1851   pr 8-p 551

   Guardian - Josiah Gilbert

IDLEBUS, John   W-1850   pr 8-p 451
   wife - Margaret   Union Twp.
   daus - Christina Foyers, Mary Peterson & their heirs
       Margaret Young & Malinda Geig

   No exr named in will

JACKSON, Beulah   E-1824   pr 2-p 498
    Admr - Robert Williamson   pr 3-p 137
                                                    Marietta

JAMES, George   E-1844   pr 7-p 57, 58, 391, 501
    Admr - Samuel W. Smith   Wesley Twp.

JARVIS, Peter   W-1845   pr 7-p 248
    wife - unnamed   Roxbury Twp.
    sons - Lyman & George
    daus - Jane Acheson, Elizabeth Stiles
    son-in-law - Daniel Van Clief

    Exrs - Lyman Jarvis & George Jarvis

JENCKES, Rebecca Carter   W-1840   pr 6-p 107
    (of Providence, R.I. where will
    was proved, 1837)

    sons - Francis Carter Jenckes &
           Amos Throop Jenckes
    daus of sister, Elizabeth Ann Danforth,
           wife of Walter R. Danforth

    Exr - Charles F. Tillinghast

JENKINS, Evan   E-1847   pr 8-p 8, 91
    wife - Amy   Roxbury Twp.
    minor ch - Evan J. & Samuel B.
    bound girl - Marthas Ellis

    Admr - Hiram Gard

JENNINGS, Jonathan   E-1808   pr 1-p 164, 199, 287
    widow - Elizabeth Jennings   Marietta
    9 heirs, each of whom gets a share at settlement
    1. Zebulon Jennings for himself and 2. Jeniah,
    his ward; 3. George Nixon and Margaret, his
    wife; 4. Otis Record & Nancy, his wife; &
    to William Hill, guardian of: 5. Delila;
    6. Elizabeth;'7. Jonathan; 8. Henry; &
    9. Rhoda Jennings

    Admx - widow - Elizabeth Jennings became
                   Elizabeth Nixon before settlement
                   (husband - William Nixon)
                   (Marriage - 23 December, 1810

JETT, Dr. Thomas   E-1832   pr 5-p 11, 16, 329
    Admx - Mary Jett (widow)   Marietta Twp.

JOHNSON, Aaron   E-1855   pr 9-p 607
    widow - Caroline   B-256
    minor dau - Caroline

    Admr - Enos S. Chapman

```
JOHNSON, George              E-1852            pr 9-p 172, 179, 180, 479
   brothers & sisters of full age - William,    B-27, 82
   Roena, Samaria and Elizabeth Johnson         Warren Twp.
   minors - Bloomfield, Joseph and Jacob Johnson

   Admr - William Johnson


JOHNSON, James               E-1798            pr 1-p 35, 37, 38
   Admr - George Johnson, then                  Newtown Twp. - now
   Admr de bonis non - Valentine Johnson        a Twp. in Muskingum Co.,OH
                   one of heirs 1800


JOHNSON, Jonas               W-1816            pr 1-p 294, 296
   wife - Ruth                                  Marietta
   son - a minor under age 21 - Perly
   daus - Amy, Lydia Ann, & Mary, all under 18

   Execx - wife, Ruth


JOHNSON, Ruth                E-1823            pr 3-p 81
   Admr - P. B. Johnson


JOHNSON, Moses               E-1814            pr 1-p 273, 315
   Admx - neglected to sign                     Union Twp.


JOLLY, Albert G.             W-1830            pr 4-p 324, 362, 363, 588
   wife - Ethelinda                             Ludlow Twp.
   2 minor children, not named

   Exr - Henry Jolly (father)


JOLLY, William H.            W-1839            pr 6-p 25
   wife - Cynthia                               Belpre Twp.
   children - but no names

   Execx - wife, Cynthia


*JONES, Edward W.            G-1851            pr 8-p 598
   son of E. W. Jones, dec'd                    B-156
   accts. show ward rec'd portion also of estate of
   John Henton, dec'd

   Guardian - Thomas Henton


JONES, John Coffin, Jr.      W-1830            pr 4-p 345, 527
   wife - Elizabeth (2nd wife)
   (testator of Boston, Mass. where will probated 1829)
   2 daus - by first wife
   5 daus and son - John Coffin, Jr.

   Execx - wife, Elizabeth Jones


JONES, Thomas                E-1850            pr 8-p 426, 428
   widow and one minor child                    B-273

   Admr - Joseph Jones
```

JOY, Benjamin   W-1831   pr 4-p 441
(of Boston, Mass. where will probated 1829)

    wife - Hannah
    brother - Charles Joy and wife, Elizabeth
    son - Joseph B. Joy
    other children not named, but shares of dau
    to be in trust

    Execx - wife, Hannah

JUDGE, William   W-1849   pr 8-p 274, 327, 329, 563
    wife - not named   Jolly Twp.
    sons - Michiel, James, Samuel
    daus - Nancy, Ruth, Polly & Eunice

    Exr - James Judge (but John Hensel declined)

JUDSON, Abigail   W-1845   pr 7-p 140
(widow of Plymouth, Mass. where
will was probated 1842)

    dau - Abigail B.
    son - Adoniram

    Execx - Abigail E. Judson (dau)

JUDSON, Adoniram   W-1832   pr 4-p 579
(of Plymouth, Mass. where will was probated 1827)

    wife - Abigail
    dau - Abigail Brown Judson
    sons - Adoniram, now missionary in India, Elnathan

    Execx - wife - Abigail Judson

JUDSON, William   E-1822   pr 2-p 344, 360
    Admx - Elizabeth Judson, widow   Marietta

KEHOE, Ann   W-1852   pr 9-p 199
    mother - Mary Johnson   B-40
    sisters - Matilda and Amanda Johnson   Belpre Twp

    Exr - Abraham Johnson (brother)

KERR, Charles   W-1845   pr 7-p 256, 280, 293, 315
    wife - Jane   Newport Twp.
    daus - Margaret Reese, Jane Brown
    son - Jonathan
    grandch - Charles F. & Phebe J. McKibben

    Exr - Benjamin Rightmire

KESSELRING, George   E-1846   pr 7-p 338
    Admx - Elizabeth Kesselring (wife)

KEYLER, Conrad   E-1790   pr 1-p 5
   (soldier in service of U.S.)

   Admr - Capt. David Zeigler

KIDD, Hannah   E-1839   pr 5-p 596
   Admr - Thomas Kidd   Fearing Twp.

KIDD, Nathaniel   W-1824   pr 3-p 157, 238, 347
   (also Nathan)   pr 4-p 250
   wife - Hannah   Fearing Twp.
   children unnamed in will, but one is John
      mentioned in settlement

   Admr - with will annexed - Jesse Hill

KIDWELL, James   E-1842   pr 6-p 401, 402
   widow - Margaret later mar. ____ Pugh and   pr 7-p 583
      was gdn. of Louisa Kidwell   Barlow Twp.

   Admr - Walter Kidwell

*KIDWELL, Louisa   G-1846   pr 7-p 392
   dau of James Kidwell   pr 8-p 292

   Guardian was her mother, Margaret, who
        later married _____ Pugh

KINGSBURY, Jacob   W-1837   pr 5-p 414
   (of Franklin, Conn. in New London Co.
   where will probated in 1837)

   wife - Sallie P. Kingsbury
   children - James Wilkinson Kingsbury; (2) Julia
            Ann Ellis Hartshorn; (3) Thomas Humphrey
            Cushing Kingsbury; (4) William Eustis
            Kingsbury; (5) Sarah Hill Kingsbury; &
            Charles Ellis Kingsbury

   Admr - John Manning of Lebanon

KINNE, Nathan   E-1808   pr 1-p 121, 122, 182
   widow   Adams Twp.

   Admr - Enoch Wing

KINSMAN, Jeremiah   W-1839   pr 6-p 22
   (of Plainfield, Conn., Windham Co.
   where will probated 1832)

   dau - Sarah Adams
   son-in-law Roswell Adams
   dau - Joanna Bacon, wife of Benjamin Bacon and
      her children

   Exr - Roswell Adams (son-in-law)

KIRBY, Thomas   E-1837   pr 5-p 426, 427
    Admx - Rebecca Kirby (wife)   Roxbury Twp.

KNIGHT, Michael   E-1790   pr 1-p 5
    Soldier in service of U.S.
    Admx - Mary Knight, widow of dec'd

KNOWLES, Jesse   W-1840   pr 6-p 115, 345
    youngest son - Sylvester B. Knowles   Belpre Twp.
    eldest dau - Cynthia A. Guthrie
    youngest dau - Esther R. Knowles

    Exr - Sylvester B. Knowles

KNOWLES, Leander   E-1834   pr 5-p 223, 278
    Admx - Frances M. Knowles   Belpre Twp.

KNOWLTON, Daniel   W-1849   pr 8-p 249, 272
    (also NOLTON)   Ludlow Twp.

    wife - Lyda (Lydia)
    11 children - William R. Knowlton, Sarah Cline,
                  Anes Smith; Abner C., Andrew C.,
                  Elizabeth A., Esau, Rachel, Emly,
                  Daniel & Mary J. Knowlton

    Execx - Lydia Knowlton - wife

KNOWLTON, William   W-1828   pr 4-p 212, 232, 377
    wife - Isabel Knowlton   Ludlow Twp.
    children - Zerviah, Cavin, William,
               Luther, Robert & John

    Exr - son - John(wife also named in will
                 but did not serve)

KNOWLTON, William   E-1842   pr 6-p 357, 358
    widow - Elizabeth Knowlton   pr 7-p 20, 31
    children - but no names   Ludlow Twp.

    Admr - George Freemyer

LAFLIN, John   E-1852   pr 9-p 157, 158
    Admr - Harley Laflin   B-12
                                                 Watertown Twp.

LAKE, Archibald   E-1800   pr 1-p 38, 41
    Admr - Andrew Lake   Adams Twp.

LAKE, Caroline   W-1848   pr 8-p 177, 220, 231, 423
    Aunt - Deborah Lake   Watertown Twp.
    Exr - Seth Woodford

```
LAKE, Emaline                   W-1845          pr 7-p 253, 283, 284, 314
  (also Emeline)                                pr 8-p 112
  father - Peter B. Lake                        Wesley Twp.
  grandfather - Thomas Lake
  mother - Catharine Lake; Aunt, Deborah Lake
  brother - James Lake
  sisters - Caroline and Lidie Lake

  Exr - Peter B. Lake


LANCASTER, Thomas               W-1846          pr 7-p 346, 445, 447
  wife                                          Salem Twp.
  daus - Elizabeth Clay; Rachel Pixley;
      Nancy Delong, Mary Scovill
  sons - Benjamin, James & David Lancaster

  Exr - James R. Lancaster (David also named but
                   did not serve)


LANG, Daniel                    E-1852          pr 9-p 322
  widow - Caroline and children                 B-56
                                                Fearing Twp.
  Admr - George Stanley


LANKFORD, Stephen               W-1850          pr 8-p 515, 547
  wife - Ann                                    Fearing Twp.
  sons - Joseph, Thomas, James
  daus - Ann Elizabeth Stanley, Patience Lane
      and Mary Lankford

  Exrs - wife Ann Lankford & son, Joseph Lankford


LAWRENCE, John                  W-1837          pr 5-p 352
  (late of New York City where will
   proved 1810)

  John - son by 1st marriage
  Mary & Elizabeth by 1st marriage
  Emily, Francis & Margaret, 3 ch. of 2nd marriage
  Ann - wife of George W. Hawkes

  Exr - bro-in-law - William Tilgham of Phila. & 3
        friends of N.Y.C. - Egbert Benson, Matthew Clarkson
        & Egbert Benson, Jr.


LAWRENCE, John McDougal         W-1837          pr 5-p 355
  (of N.Y. City where will proved 1835)

  sister - Elizabeth Lawrence to receive all estate

  Execx - sister, Elizabeth Lawrence


LAWRENCE, Romeo                 E-1827          pr 4-p 142
  Admx - Pamela Lawrence, widow                 Waterford Twp.
```

```
LAWRENCE, Rufus              E-1834              pr 5-p 133, 279, 407
    widow - Rebecca who mar. Benjamin Hart of   Waterford Twp.
      Watertown before settlement
    3 children - minors - Henderson, Minerva,
              and Sarah (but Minerva also called Almira)

    Admr - Samson K. White


LAWSON, James                E-1793              pr 1-p 11
    Admr - John Matthews of Gallipolis, a creditor   Gallipolis Twp.
                                                  (now Gallia Co.)


LAWTON, Peter                E-1850              pr 8-p 382, 385, 387
    widow & 1 child not named                    pr 9-p 167
                                                  Watertown Twp.
    Admr - George Bowen


*LEACH, Lucy                 G-1832              pr 5-p 565
    (alias BENT, Lucy)
    See also will of Daniel Bent, her father who
    names her his natural dau by Deborah Leach (pr4-p130)

    Guardian - Nahum Bent


LEACH, Thomas                E-1843              pr 6-p 450
    Admr - William Leach                         Waterford Twp.


LEAVENS, Elizabeth           E-1830              pr 4-p 417, 592
    children - Matilda E. Leavens of full age    Belpre Twp.
              & minors, Esther & Catherine

    Admx - Matilda E. Leavens


LEAVENS, Joseph              E-1815              pr 1-p 290
    (also LEVENS)                                pr 2-p 29
                                                  pr 4-p 128
    widow - Elizabeth                            Belpre Twp.
    children - Henry (of age in 1827) and
    minors - Evelina, Matilda, Catherine & Esther

    Admx - Elizabeth Leavens
    Admr - Stephen Guthrie


LEEDHAM, John G.             E-1851              pr 8-p 604, 608
    widow - Anna A.                              pr 9-p 212
    minor child - Wm Henry                       B-39

    Admr - William H. Stewart


LEFAVOUR, Nathaniel          E-1820              pr 2-p 200, 201, 208
    (of Salem, Mass.)

    Admr - Moses McFarland of Marietta, Ohio
```

LEFFINGWELL, Cristopher   W-1839   pr 6-p 15
    (of Norwich, Conn., New London Co., where
    will proved 1810)

    dau - Lucretia Connell & her children;
    children of dec'd dau., Lydia (late wife of
        John Whiting of Canaan, N.Y.); Christopher,
        William & Elizabeth Leffingwell;
    Joanna Lathrop, wife of Charles, and Jerusha Leffingwell

    Exr - William Leffingwell

LEFFINGWELL, William   W-1839   pr 6-p 16
    (of New Haven, Conn. where will
    probated in 1834)

    1. 5 heirs are ch. of late son, William C. Leffingwell
    2. dau Caroline, wife of Augustus R. Street
    3. dau Maria S. Williams, widow of Timothy Dwight Williams
    4. son Lucius W. Leffingwell
    5. also leaves trust for son, Edward H. Leffingwell

    Exrs - Roger S. Baldwin, Samuel I. Hitchcock and
           Henry White

LEGET, Samuel   W-1832   pr 4-p 600
    bros - James, Henry, William & Robert   pr 5-p 19, 210
    mother - Sarah Featherston   Waterford Twp.
    nephew - Samuel Leget

    Exr - Robert Leget

LEGET, Wesley F.   E-1849   pr 8-p 257, 273
    (also Legett or Legget)   pr 9-p 348

    heirs - Lorenzo D. Leget, Rufus Leget, Samuel   Waterford Twp.
        Leget & Robert Leget, gdn of Lundy
        & Frederick Leget

    Admr - Ebenezer B. Leget

LEGGIT, John   E-1805   pr 1-p 85
    (LIGGET)   Waterford Twp.

LEGIT, John Jr.   E-1821   pr 2-p 206, 249
                                                       Waterford Twp.

LEIPER, Thomas   W-1838   pr 5-p 453
    (of Philadelphia, Pa. where
    will probated, 1825)

    wife - Elizabeth
    9 children - 3 sons - George, William & Samuel
                 dau - Martha & husband, Rev. Dr. Janeway
                 dau - Elizabeth & husband, Robert Taylor
                 dau - Helen, husband, Dr. Robert M. Patterson
                 dau - Jane Duvall & husband, not named
                 2 daus - Ann Grey Leiper & Julia Dunlap Leiper
    Exrs - wife, Elizabeth, sons, George & William, and
           friends, Paul Beck, Jr. & Joseph Reed

```
LEONARD, William B.              E-1807          pr 1-p 128, 148
                                                 Marietta
    Admx - Lydia Fulton

LESURE, Nicholas                 E-1795          pr 1-p 14
                                                 Gallipolis Twp.
    Admr - John Nicholas Petit, Esq.             (now in Gallia Co., O.)

LEVINS, John (also LEVENS)       E-1798          pr 1-p 35
    Admx - Easter Levins                         Belpre Twp.
    Admr - Joseph Levins

LEWIS, Elizabeth                 E-1849          pr 8-p 441, 442, 459
    Admr - John Crawford

LEWIS, Solomon                   E-1847          pr 8-p 93, 95, 278
    widow - unnamed                              Union Twp.
    Admr - Anthony Hill

LIENGME, Florien L.              E-1849          pr 8-p 226, 228, 232, 519
    (also, Leingme)                              B-322, 323
    widow - Julia
    minor children - Emily & Henrietta

    Admr - Eugene Pierrot

LIGHTFRITZ, John                 E-1841          pr 6-p 229
    widow -                                      pr 8- p 201
    3 children - under 15 years - all got yr's support  Warren Twp.
    Admr - John Crawford
LINCOLN, Joseph                  E-1808          pr 1-p 130, 265
    widow - Frances                              Marietta

*LINN, Elizabeth                 G-1850          pr 8-p 521
    Guardian - Henry Winland

LISK, John                       W-1831          pr 4-p 448, 494, 495
    wife - Elizabeth                             pr 5-p 30
    son - Nicholas P. Lisk                       Grandview Twp.
    relation not stated - Samuel Lisk

    Exr - Nicholas P. Lisk

LITTLE, Keziah                   W-1814          pr 1-p 255, 287
    3 daus - Lydia Cram, Christian Tisdall
        & Lucy Cotton
    17 grandchildren:  not copied here, but 6 are children of
        only son , Nathaniel, dec'd 1810

    Admr - Aaron Waldo Putnam (named Exr had died)

LITTLE, Nathaniel                E-1810          pr 1-p 184, 191, 196,
    Children:  Wealthy Little, wife of Ira Hill, Jr.,      197, 309
               Charles, Henry, Lewis, Nathaniel, Jr., pr 4-p 620
               & George Little                   Newport Twp.

    Admr - Luther Dana (died 1814), then
    Admr de bonis non - William Dana
```

```
LIVERMORE, Jonas            E-1823              pr 2-p 318, 382
                            (May)               pr 3-p 555
     4 children - 3 of age by 1830: Jonas, Jr.  pr 4-p 254, 468
          of Marietta; Oliver of Illinois;      Marietta
          & Andrew of Marietta; 1 minor -
          Mary, with gnd., Ebenezer Gates

     Admr - Abel Prescott, who died, then
     Admr de bonis non - Jonas Livermore, Jr.


LIVERMORE, Molly            E-1823              pr 2-p 448
                            (Nov.)              pr 3-p 443
     Admr - Jonas Livermore, Jr.                Marietta


LIVINGSTON, Brockholst      W-1830              pr 4-p 312
     (of New York City where will
      probated 1823)
      wife - Mrs. Livingston
      sister - Judith Watkins
      4 sons - Carroll, Anson, Henry Brockholst,
          and Jasper Hall Livingston
      4 daus - Eliza, wife of Jasper Hall Livingston,
          Catharine Augusta McVicker, wife of Archibald,
          Susan French Ledyard, Catharine Louise Livingston

     Exr - Susan French Ledyard


LOBDELL, Henry              E-1845              pr 7-p 290, 292
                                                pr 8-p 138, 151
     wife also dead by settlement in 1848
     since expenses include coffins for H. Lobdell and wife

     Admr - Lewis Lobdell


LOCKARD, Joseph             E-1805              pr 1-p 87
                                                Marietta


LOOMIS, Libbeus             W-1837              pr 5-p 338
     (of Cherry Valley, N.Y.,
      Otsego Co., where will probated, 1836)
      Many legatees - mostly sisters & brothers,
                not copied here

     Exr - David H. Little


LORING, Daniel              W-1823              pr 2-p 435
     widow - Lucy                               pr 3-p 99
     dau - Mary Beebe                           pr 4-p 167
     sons - Israel & Ezekiel How Loring,        Belpre Twp.
          Jesse & Oliver Rice Loring
     heirs of dau., Charlotte Putnam;
     grandson - William Beebe
     granddaughters - Mary Beebe & Elizabeth Putnam

     Exr - O. R. Loring
```

```
*LORING, Francis A.          G-1848              pr 8-p 183 to 185
        William W.                               B-51
        Austin T.
        Mary C.
    These are minor children of Jesse Loring

    Guardian - Maria Loring

LORING, Jesse               E-1843              pr 7-p 31, 40, 360
                                                Belpre Twp.
    Admr - Oliver R. Loring

LUCAS, Samuel               E-1818              pr 2-p 64, 89
                                                Roxbury Twp.
    Admrs - Mary Lucas & Daniel Coalman

*LUDEMAN, Conrad            G-1845              pr 7-p 198, 476
    (lunatic)                                   Fearing Twp.

    Guardian - Thomas F. Stanley

LUND, Abigail               W-1845              pr 7-p 175
    (widow of Isaac Lund)                       Aurelius Twp.
    daus - Sarah Abigail Doan, Mary Danforth,
        Nancy Ann & Catharine Lund
    grandson - Charles Doan, son of Sarah Abigail

    Exr - Isaac Taylor Lund (son)

LUND, Isaac                 W-1837              pr 5-p 356
                                                pr 6-p 470
    wife - Abigail Lund                         Aurelius Twp.
    daus - Sarah Abigail, Mary Danforth,
        Nancy Ann, Susan & Catharine Lund
    son - Isaac Taylor Lund

    Execx - wife, Abigail Lund

LYONS, Randolph             E-1841              pr 6-p 178
                                                Waterford Twp.
    Admr - John Lyons

McALLISTER, William         E-1818              pr 2-p 119,121, 172
                                                Marietta
    Admx - Nancy McAllister

McCABE, Robert              E-1823              pr 2-p 488, 494
                                                pr 3-p 320, 430
    wife dec'd about same time, it shows        Marietta
    in bills for last sickness
    children of age - Hannah Jennings, wife
    of Junia Jennings
    6 minors - Jacob C., Patience Q., Robert, Polly,
        Lorenzo D., & John W. McCabe

    Admr - Junia Jennings

McCANDLISH, Anthony         E-1824              pr 3-p 240, 244, 246
    Children got allowance for yr's support,   pr 4-p 46, 471
    minor heirs - George McCandlish (gdn - Samuel   Waterford Twp.
                Black), William & Elizabeth
                (gdn - Robert McCandlish)

    Admrs - A(anselm) T. Nye & George Bowen
                                    Washington County, Ohio Probate-85-
```

McCLINTICK, Catherine   W-1828   pr 4-p 180
    son - Samuel & 2 daus mentioned in will,   pr 5-p 109 (petition-1832)
    (Katherine & Rachel), In petition   Marietta
    to sell land, the minor, Rachel is rep-
    resented by her bro. & gdn., William
    Tilden McClintick who had bought out the
    share of bro. James McClintick of Chillicothe.

    Exr - son, Samuel McClintick

McCLINTICK, Samuel   E-1815   pr 1-p 312, 313
    Admr - Stephen Otis   Marietta

McCLINTOCK, Mary   W-1849   pr 8-p 345
    husband - William H. McClintock   Marietta Twp.
    dau - Elizabeth Jameson

    Exr - named in will was Robert T. Miller who declined

McCLUER, John   W-1827   pr 4-p 104
    wife - Hannah   Roxbury Twp.
    sons - John, Orange, Chester, Thomas, & Alexander
    daus - Sally & Hannah

    Exr - son, Thomas McCluer

McCLUNIE, Michael   E-1824   pr 3-p 82, 305
    Admr - John Mills   Marietta

McCOLLUM, Daniel   E-1847   pr 8-p 52, 61, 100
    Dau - Nancy True (claimed chest)   pr 9-p 124, 165

    Admr - Israel Brown, followed by
    Admr de bonis non - Charles Algeo

McCONNEL, Talbot   W-1839   pr 6-p 23, 64
                                                   Wesley Twp.
    father- Edward McConnel
    grandfather - David Townsend's estate
    cousin - Sarah Collwell
    bros. - James & Townsend

    Exrs - Edward McConnel (Father) &
           Townsend McConnel (brother)

McCOY, Alexander   E-1823   pr 2-p 414, 416
                                                   pr 3-p 314
    wife - Elizabeth, who later mar. ___   pr 4-p 116
        Hagerman   Waterford Twp.
    children - Letticia Greenman (wife of Jeremiah
            Greenman, Jr.), Elizabeth McCoy,
            Jane Marks (wife of John Marks) of full age,
            & minors - Matilda, Hiram & Alexander McCoy

    Admrs - Ami Lawrence & Jeremiah Greenman, Jr.

*McCOY, Joshua   G-1854   pr 9-p 537
      minor, age 12, son of George McCoy dec'd
      petition by guardian to sell ward's undivided 1/3 part of
      land in Noble Co, together with that of his sister,
      Rebecca Ann

      Guardian - Michael Feltner

*McCOY, Rebecca Ann   G-1854   pr 9-p 534
      minor, age 16 yr., dau of George McCoy dec'd   B-172
      petition by guardian to sell ward's undivided
      1/3 part of land in Noble Co. with that of her
      brother, Joshua

      Guardian - Michael Feltner

McDONALD, Daniel   W-1843   pr 7-p 11
      had 11 children by 3 wives: 1 by first,
      5 each by other two
      by 1st wife, Sally - George
      by 2nd wife, Elizabeth - James, William.Henrietta,
                              Elizabeth & Nancy
      by 3rd wife, Catharine - Mary Ann Sherlock, Sally McDonald,
                              Mariah, Wallace & Isaac

      No exr named

McDONALD, James   E-1798   pr 1-p 32
                                                   Belpre Twp.

McELHINNY, Joseph   E-1840   pr 6-p 140, 143
      widow - Mary   Lawrence Twp.
      5 children

      Admx - Mary McElhinny (widow)

McGINNIS, Margaret   E-1849   pr 8-p 374, 381, 574

      Admr - Richard Scott at Ludlow Twp.

McGONEGAL, Daniel   E-1816   pr 1-p 308
      Admr - Truman Ransom   pr 2-p 66, 82
                                                   Adams Twp.

*McGOWAN, William Dana   G-1835   pr 5-p 240
      (heir of late Jonathan Stone)
      Guardian, Peter M. McGowan whose agent,
      George Dana, petitioned to sell land.
      The ward's interest in sd estate is ¼ of
      1/6 part, an undivided interest in lands
      set apart as dower for widow of Jonathan
      Stone, sold to John Stone.

McINTOSH, John   E-1821   pr 2-p 280
     widow got allowance for yr's support,   pr 3-p 120
     not named   Marietta
Admr - John McIntosh

McINTOSH, Nathan   E-1823   pr 3-p 76, 170
     widow - Rhoda   pr 4-p 430, 507
     children - Enoch S. of Morgan Co.,   pr 5-p 111, 123, 135
     William M., Nathan H., Lucy & Samuel D   Marietta
     McIntosh*; also, minor children of Rhoda Ann
     Chamberlain, dec'd, namely, Gurden &
     Lucy Chamberlain whose natural gdn. is
     Judah M. Chamberlain

Admr - John Clark

     *by April, 1830, in 2nd petition, Samuel D. McIntosh
     was deceased and his heirs, all minors, were -
     Rhoda Sophia, Samuel Lewis McIntosh whose natural
     gdn was Deborah S. McIntosh

McINTOSH, Samuel D.   E-1830   pr 4-p 415, 575
                                                         Marietta
     widow - Deborah
     minor children - Rhoda Sophia McIntosh
                      Samuel Lewis McIntosh

Admr - Milton Foster

McKAWEN, Charles   W-1820   pr 2-p 185, 463, 562
                                                         pr 3-p 544
     wife - Liddy   pr 4-p 27
     children mentioned, not named   Marietta
     prob. grandchildren - Joanna & Angeline
     Lincoln, children of Obediah Lincoln

     Exr - Obediah Lincoln who died before administering, so
     Admr - John Merrill was apptd, Nov., 1822

McKEWAN, Lydia   W-1823   pr 2-p 423
                                                         pr 3-p 35, 37, 40, 298
     brother - Edmund Moulton   Marietta
     children of sister - Mary Bond, namely
     Enoch Bond & Nancy Plummer
     grandson - of bro. Joseph Moulton, that is
                Joseph Haskell

     Admr - Benjamin Corp (appt after named Exrs refused)

McNEAL, James   E-1808   pr 1-p 167, 246
     Admr - John McNeal (prob. the one   pr 2-p 212, 231, 256
            with estate 1819) then,   Adams Twp.
     Admx - Anna McNeal, relation not stated

McNEAL, John   E-1819   pr 2-p 182, 198
     Admx - Anna McNeal   Wooster Twp. (early name
                                                            for Watertown Twp.)

McNUTT, Jane   W-1845   pr 7-p 177, 231, 317
   (widow of James McNutt, late of   Union Twp.
   Harrison Co., Ohio)
   dau - Sophia Willis
   sons - James & Joseph
   grandchildren - heirs of Benjamin McNutt

   Exr - James Willis, son-in-law

McPEEK, Benjamin   E-1852   pr 9-p 208, 297
(McPeck)   B-35
   only heir - dau, age 5 yrs., Nancy Ellen   Lawrence Twp.

   Admr - Elias O. Lennington

McVAY, John   W-1823   pr 2-p 422, 499
   wife - Elizabeth   pr 3-p 283
   daus - Polly Hix, Levinah, Syntha   Grandview Twp.
   sons - Samuel & Henry

   Exr - Samuel McVay, son
   Execx - Elizabeth McVay, wife

McWHORTER, Frances   W-1844   pr 7-p 63
   (widow of New York City where
   will proved 1844)
   One minor son - Alexander McWhorter
   asks Court to name Exr and tnat he be placed
   in a minister's home.

MAES   see MEES

MANBY, Samuel   E-1832   pr 4-p 580, 582
   wife - Elizabeth (dec'd by Mar., 1835)   pr 5-p 8, 214, 261
   3 minor children - Thomas, Elizabeth & Harriet   Fearing Twp.
             Manby (gdn - Joel Tuttle)

   Admrs - Tnomas Ward & Jewett Palmer

MARSH, Sarcelius   W-1850   pr 8-p 446, 547
   wife - Elizabeth   Salem Twp.
   bro - Robert Marsh
   legatee - James McCoy

   Admr - Moses True (after James McCoy named Exr did not serve)

MARTIN, George   E-1834   pr 5-p 149, 150, 305
   widow - Rebecca   pr 6-p 318
   children of age - William, John & Mary Ann   Roxbury Twp.
   minors - George, Alexander, Nancy, Rebecca, Nathaniel H.,
       Marinda, Ruth, Samantha & Nathan Martin

   Admrs - Hiram Gard & William Martin, son

MARTIN, Mary   E-1824   pr 2-p 560
    Admr - George Compton   Ludlow Twp.

MARTIN, Simeon   W-1837   pr 5-p 350
    (of Seekonk, Mass., Bristol Co., where
    will proved, 1819)
    wife - Abigail
    children - Amy Wood, Susan Stephens, Edward Martin,
              Abigail Fearing, George W. Martin, Eliza Dennie &
              Harriet Allen

    Exrs - wife, Abigail Martin & Wheeler Martin
                        (relation not given)

MARTIN, William   E-1850   pr 8-p 395, 431,
    widow - Teresser Martin   pr 9-p 365
    children - not named

    Admr - Moses Campbell

MARVIN, James   E-1834   pr 5-p 183, 311, 367
    widow - Sarah   Roxbury Twp. (at
    children - David and Jesse Marvin;   settlement, said to be
                                                    Waterford Twp.)
              Hannah Coon, wife of Sheffield Coon

    Admr - John Waterman

MASON, Gideon   W-1849   pr 8-p 251
    wife - unnamed in will but Hannah in proceedings   Jolly Twp.
    grandch - 7 children of dec'd dau, Catharine
              Powell, late consort of William Powell
    children mostly have had full share (portion)
              except John who is to get residue

    Exr - son, John Mason

MASON, John   E-1851   pr 9-p 49, 56, 72, 136,
    widow - Rosanna   360, 394
    minor ch - John S., George W., Irene J.,   B-13
              Margaret M., Franklin S. &   Adams Twp.
              Velinda L.
    ch of full age - Horatio W., Manley W.

    Admr - Henry P. Mason

MASON, William   W-1813   pr 1-p 243, 251
    (Capt. William)   Adams Twp.
    wife - Susannah
    children - unnamed except Adolphus who is to
              get horse when of age

    Execx - wife - Susannah

```
MASON, William              W-1826          pr 3-p 509
    wife - Sally                             pr 4-p 14, 16, 248
    5 daus - Polly Chidester, Jane Sprague (wife of   Adams Twp.
        George), Nancy McAtee (wife of William),
        Betsey Morris (wife of William), and
        minor, Rebecca Mason
    5 sons mentioned in will were - James, William,
        John, also, minors Henry P. & Jacob, plus,
        Isaac, born posthumously & reported later
    grandchild - James Starling

    Exr - John Mason


MATHEWS, Abel               W-1822          pr 2-p 270
                                            Union Twp.
    wife - Molly
    sons - John, Philo
    stepson - William Woodard, son of present wife
    daus - Hannah & Charlotte

    Exrs - sons, John & Philo Mathews


MATTHEWS, Benjamin          E-1846          pr 7-p 436, 447
                                            pr 8-p 349, 587
    widow - Ruth                            Roxbury Twp.
    children - not named

    Admr - John Matthews


MATTHEWS, William           E-1841          pr 6-p 271
                                            pr 8-p 351
    widow - Sarah                           Lawrence Twp.
    children but no names

    Admr - Sarah Matthews who later married
        _____Dye & was Sarah Dye at settlement


MAUPETIT, Caesar            E-1794          pr 1-p 13
                                            Gallipolis Twp.
    Admr - John Gilbert Petit, Esq.         (now in Gallia Co., O.)


*MAXON, Hiram               G-1826          pr 3-p 445 (Hiram)
    Cyrus                                   pr 3-p 471-476 (all)
    Elhanan W.      The 6 children of       pr 4-p 461 (Elhanan W.)
    Lydia           Henry & Elizabeth       pr 4-p 541 (Rufus)
    Henry Avery     Maxon (Maxson)
    Rufus

    Guardian - William R. Putnam for all to begin with
    and in addition each one except Lydia had a 2nd gdn;
    Hiram - John Miller; Cyrus - Levi Chapman; Elhanan W. -
    Walter Curtis; Henry Avery - Paul Fearing; & Rufus -
    Zebulon Jennings


MAXSON, Elizabeth           E-1815          pr 1-p 285
    (MAXON)                                 pr 3-p 116
    widow of Henry                          Fearing Twp.

    Admr - William R. Putnam
```

MAXSON, Henry   E-1812   pr 1-p 211, 235, 289
    widow - Elizabeth Maxson   Fearing Twp.
    6 children - Hiram, Cyrus, Elhanan W., Lydia,
            Henry Avery, & Rufus

    Admr - Wm Corner

MAXSON, Hiram   E-1824   pr 4-p 7
    (MAXON)
    (This is son of Henry & Elizabeth Maxson -
    see gdn. accts for Hiram Maxon and others)

    Admr - William Corner

MAXWELL, Eliza Anne   W-1845   pr 7-p 178
    Exr - husband - Samuel Maxwell   Marietta

MAXWELL, Elizabeth   W-1844   pr 7-p 67, 195
    Exr - brother - Samuel Maxwell   Marietta

MEDBERRY, Charles   E-1828   pr 4-p 262, 392, 425
    (also MEDBURY)   Belpre Twp.

    widow - Marcay Medbury
    children - minors - Abigail, Elizabeth
                        & Charles

    Admr - O. R. Loring

MEDLEY, William   W-1838   pr 5-p 481, 516
    friend (probably wife) - Eliza Payne   pr 6-p 125
    3 children of Eliza - not named   Ludlow Twp.
    ch. of dec'd dau - Metilda Derbon

    Admr apptd - Eliza Medley
            (after named Exr declined)

MEES, Charles Nelson   E-1822   pr 3-p 196
    (MEESE, Nelson)   Marietta
    Heirs are Katherine Smith, Mary Emly Meese,
            Benson Meese, Cynthia Mays, J.
            Valentine & Jonathan Meese

    Admr - Jonathan Meese

MEES, Jonathan   E-1828   pr 4-p 215, 218, 458
    (MAES)   Marietta

    Admrs- Jonathan Valentine & Horace Root

MEIGS, Ebenezer   E-1813   pr 1-p 247, 284
    Admr - William R. Putnam   Marietta

MEIGS, Return Jonathan   E-1825   pr 3-p 359
    Admx - Sophia Meigs (widow)   pr 4-p 359
                                                 Marietta

MELLEN, Richard   E-1791   pr 1-p 5
    (Soldier in service of U.S.)

    Admr - Capt David Zeigler

MELLOR, George   E-1805   pr 1-p 87
                                                   Waterford Twp.

MELLOR, Samuel   W-1850   pr 8-p 511, 537, 546
    wife - Nancy   Watertown Twp.
    youngest son - Walter H. Mellor   also given as
    youngest dau - Joann   Waterford Twp.
    eldest son - Jesse S. Mellor
    eldest dau - Susan, late wife of Hiel Dunsmoor
    second dau - Mary, wife of Volney Adams
    4th dau - Nancy Jane, wife of John Godfrey
    4 children of dec'd dau - Love Prudence, late
                             wife of Joel Adams

    Exr - Smith Green

MELVIN, Isaac   W-1845   pr 7-p 250
                                                   Roxbury Twp.
wife - Abigail
    daus - Eliza Ann Shrader, Louisa Green
    grandson - Isaac Melvin, son of Charles Melvin, dec'd

    Exr - Henry P. Dearborn of Windsor, Morgan Co., Ohio

MENCHAN, Michael   W-1850   pr 8-p 404
                                                   Union Twp.
    mentions wife (unnamed)
    and father's estate in Germany

    No Exr named

MEREDITH, New   E-1852   pr 9-p 391, 392, 463, 562
    widow - Dorcas   B-53, 80, 410
    children of full age - Betsey, wife of Richard Liberty Twp.
        McPeak of Noble Co.; Mahala, wife of Thomas J.
        Law; Susan, wife of John Cline, Lydia Meredith,
        John Meredith of Washington Co.
    minor children - New, Nancy & Rachel Meredith

    Admr - John Meredith

MERIBAN, Peter Adrian   E-1840   pr 6-p 71
    widow & children unnamed but got yr's   Marietta
        allowance - all assets for support

    no Admr named

*MERO, Ira   G-1834   pr 5-p 141

    Guardian - Walter Hall

MERRIAM, Reuben   E-1823   pr 2-p 288, 464
                                                   pr 3-p 548
    Admr - Selden N. Merriam   Adams Twp.

                              Washington County, Ohio Probate -93-

MIDDLESWART, Clark   E-1847   pr 8-p 86, 89, 100
    family   Newport Twp.

    Admx - Cynthia W. Middleswart, widow

MILES, Benjamin   E-1818   pr 2-p 75, 77, 94
    7 heirs, all of full age - Joseph B., Benjamin   pr 4-p 337
        H., and William M. Miles; Bial Stedman   B-277, 278
        (in right of wife, Mary P.); Barzilla T.,   Belpre Twp.
        Solomon S., and Rufus W. Miles

    Admrs - Benjamin H. Miles & S. S. Miles

MILLARD, Joseph T.   E-1852   pr 9-p 322, 379, 501
    widow - Lavina   B-58, 101
    children - Nathaniel P. Millard of St. Marys   Union Twp.
        Parish, Louisiana; Joseph D. and Frances
        E. Millard of Lorain Co., Ohio;
        Lavina W. Tanner dec'd, late of Greenup,
        Ky who left Julius Tanner & Alice A.
        Tanner now residing in Washington Co.;
        and John P. Millard of Washington Co.

    Admx - Lavina Millard, wife

MILLER, Amos   E-1812   pr 1-p 237
    3 minor ch - Julia, Augusta & Octavius pr 2-p 17, 18
                                            pr 3-p 440
    Admx - Mary Miller, widow   Marietta

*MILLER, Austin   G-1850   pr 8-p 470
MILLER, Vesta

    (minor children of David Miller, dec'd)

    Guardian - Isaac Perry

MILLER, David   E-1839   pr 6-p 72, 73
    widow   pr 8-p 132, 348
    children -   Wesley Twp.

    Admr - Oliver Miller, Jr. (E-1840)
    Admr de bonis non - Hapgood Goddard

MILLER, George   E-1845   pr 7-p 198, 199
    Admr - Andrew Twiggs   pr 8-p 150
                                            Salem Twp.

MILLER, John   E-1823   pr 2-p 291, 395
    Admr - John Merrill   pr 4-p 78
                                            Marietta

MILLER, John   W-1841   pr 6-p 177
    dau - Catharine T. Gates   Marietta Twp.

    Exr - Robert T. Miller (son)

MILLER, Mary   W-1850   pr 8-p 449, 540
    heirs - Patrick Campbell, John D. Amlin   pr 9-p 94
        & James M. Amlin   Fearing Twp.
    also mentioned - Mary Ann Amlin, wife of
        John D.; Eliza Amlin, wife of James M.;
    also, Mary Ann & Adeliza, daus of John D. Amlin;
        and Archibald Skinner, eldest son of John
        D. Amlin

    Exr - John D. Amlin

MILLER, Oliver, Jr.   E-1840   pr 6-p 74, 132
    widow & children got support for 1 year   pr 9-p 63
    Admr - Joseph Tilton, then   Wesley Twp.
    Admr de bonis non - John D. Chamberlain

MILLER, William   E-1840   pr 6-p 442 (settlement)
    Jour C. CPleas v. 8, p 512, 516*; v 9, p 33,   Warren Twp.
        75, 341
    Deeds - v 33, p 466 (states he was from Warren Twp.);
        * heirs unknown (see JCCP, v 8, p 516)

    Admr - John Crawford

MILLER, William   W-1844   pr 7-p 55
    wife - Mary   Fearing Twp.

    See also Jour CC P v 9, p 456 (attic)

    Exr - John D. Amlin

MINER, Matthew   E-1824   pr 2-p 445
    Admr - Henry P. Miner   pr 3-p 101

MINER, Richard   E-1816   pr 1-p 312
    Admrs - Leicester G. Converse & Esther Miner   pr 2-p 137
                                          Waterford Twp.

MIXER, Isaac   W-1815   pr 1-p 272
    son - Isaac Mixer   pr 2-p 9
    grandch - Mary, Elizabeth, William, Thomas,   pr 4-p 206
        Lewis, Harriet & Almond Mixer   Marietta
    also, Sarah Wiseman & Sarah Gilmore,
        reputed daughter

    Exr - Levi Barber

MIXER, Isaac   W-1846   pr 7-p 382
    wife, only heir, is not named   Marietta

    Exr - Ethan H. Allen

MOORE, George   E-1853   pr 9-p 344, 360, 614
    only surviving child - William   B-65, 196
    only other heir - Catherine Moore, minor,   Marietta
               dau of David Moore

    Admr - William Moore

MOORE, Patience   W-1834   pr 5-p 119, 147, 232
    Exr - Jonas Moore (husband)   Marietta Twp.

MOORE, Ruandrew   E-1849   pr 8-p 368
    widow   pr 9-p 123
    Admr - Elias O. Lennington   Liberty Twp.

MOORE, William   E-1844   pr 7-p 124, 125
    Admrs - Samuel S. Moore &   pr 8-p 468
             John M. Moore   Roxbury Twp.

MORELAND, Horatio   W-1850   pr 8-p 516
    wife - Jane
    granddau - Maryan Elizabeth Riggs
    dau of H. R. Riggs & E. Riggs
    daus - Elizabeth and Nancy Riggs

    No exr named

MORRIS, Amos   E-1823   pr 2-p 364
    Admr - Amos Wilson   pr 3-p 558
                                   Adams Twp.

MORRIS, Ann   W-1814   pr 1-p 255, 282
    sons - William & Jesse   Adams Twp.

    Exr - William Morris

MORRIS, John   W-1847   pr 7-p 473
    (colored man)   Fearing Twp.
    son - Thomas Carter Morris
    daus - Susan Pharaugh, Matilda Morris,
        & Catherine Morris Ilynteen

MORRIS, John C. A.   W-1848   pr 8-p 102
    children - mentioned but not named   Waterford Twp.

    Execx - Betsey Morris (wife)

*MORRIS, Lucetta   G-1846   pr 7-p 312
    Present Guardian - Ely Vaughn
    Former Guardian - Amos Wilson

MORRIS, Mordecai   E-1844   pr 7-p 109, 110, 140, 310
    Admr - Robert Way   pr 8-p 188
                                   Wesley Twp.

```
MORRIS, Obediah                 E-1823          pr 2-p 367, 368
    Admr - Amos Wilson                          pr 3-p 287
                                                Adams Twp.

MORRIS, Orrin N.                E-1843          pr 7-p 28, 30, 358
    Admrs - James M. Starlin & Elijah Sprague   Adams Twp.

MORRIS, Richard F.              E-1844          pr 7-p 95, 97, 114
                                                pr 8-p 234
    widow - Martha R. Morris                    pr 9-p 588
    2 minor ch - Josepn T. & Mary Ann           B-220, 232
    3 other ch (not named)                      Wesley Twp.

    Admrs - Jeremiah Morris & Martha R. Morris

MORRIS, Rufus Gilman            E-1850          pr 8-p 392, 394, 431
                                                pr 9-p 237
    minor child - Sylvester                     Adams Twp. (also given
    Admx - Caroline Morris (widow)              as Union Twp.)
    Admr - George Beebe

MORRIS, William                 E-1825          pr 3-p 349
                                                pr 4-p 33
    widow - Hannah (got ½)                      Adams Twp.
    heirs - not named (got ½)

    Admx - Hannah Morris

MORSE, Justus                   E-1823          pr 2-p 323, 326, 526
                                                pr 3-p 418
    widow - Margaret who died soon after        pr 4-p 284
    orphans - Marcellus, Rice, William and      Marietta
            Louisa Morse

    Admx - widow, Margaret; then
    Admr - Manley Morse

*MORSE, Marcellus               G-1827          pr 4-p 88, 89, 151, 512
        Rice                                        (accts of first gdn)
        William                                 pr 5-p 79, 106, 107
        Louisa                                      (accts of 2nd gdn)
    (Minor heirs of Justus Morse, dec'd)
    At settlement, ward, Louisa Morse was Louisa
        M. Babcock

    1st Guardian - Eusebius Morse
    2nd Guardian - John Crawford

MORSE, Margaret                 E-1824          pr 2-p 538, 539
    (widow of Justus Morse)                     pr 4-p 373
                                                Marietta
    Admr - Silas Cook

MORTON, William R.              E-1839          pr 6-p 65, 188, 347
                                                pr 7-p 150
    widow                                       Harmar
    children

    Admr - John Crawford
```

MOULTON, William   W-1795   pr 1-p 15, 19
    (formerly of Hampstead, N.H.   Marietta
    Rockingham County)

    wife - Lydia
    sons - Joseph & Edmund
    daus - Molley, wife of Dr. John Bond;
           Anna, Lydia & Katharine Moulton

    Exec - wife, Lydia Moulton

MULLEN, James   E-1824   pr 3-p 250, 251
                                         pr 4-p 3
    widow & 3 children (not named)   Newport Twp.

    Admr - Robert Rowland

MUNRO, Josiah   E-1801   pr 1-p 45
                                         Marietta
    Admr - Jabez True

MURDOCK, David   W-1853   pr 9-p 360, 417, 465
                                         B-73
    wife - Mary   Independence Twp.
    heirs - Hezekiah R. Riggs & wife Elizabeth;
            Squire D. Riggs & wife Nancy; John B.
            Moreland and his heirs

    Exrs - Daniel Dye & Samuel Rea

MURRY, Davidson   E-1823   pr 3-p 67, 69, 149, 310,343
    (MURRAY)   Marietta

    widow - Elizabeth
    sons - mentioned but not named

    Admr - C(aleb) Emerson

NAPIER, Archibald   E-1841   pr 6-p 216, 220
                                         pr 7-p 71, 156
    One heir was George Napier who sued, pr 8-p 354, 355
        others not named   Watertown Twp.
    Admr - Seth Woodford

NEEDHAM, Jasper   W-1851   pr 8-p 617
                                         pr 9-p 30
    wife - Beckey   Warren Twp.
    daus - Mary S. Cole, Sophronia S. Ellenwood,
           Becky Potter
    son - Jasper

    Exrs - Beckey Needham (wife) and Jasper Needham (son)

NELSON, Oliver   E-1853   pr 9-p 422, 461
                                         B-71
    Admx - Mary E. Nelson   Marietta

NESTLER, John   E-1829   pr 4-p 293
    Reports a balance is due on Govt   Watertown Twp.
    pension as of Sept., 1828

    Admr - David Fairchild

NEWTON, Oren   W-1852   pr 9-p 147, 204
    wife - Eliza (Elizabeth)   B-26
    3 unmarried ch - Emily H., Mary Frances &
                Elias Douglas Newton
    other ch - Stephen, John, Oren H..William S.,
                Elizabeth Dela Mater & Lucy L. Fuller

    Exr - John Newton - replaced by Stephen Newton as admr.

NICHOLS, James   E-1817   pr 2-p 58, 61
    widow got allowance   Marietta

    Admr - Adolphus Wing

NICKLIN, Philip Houlbrooke   W-1846   pr 7-p 348
    of Philadelphia, Pa.
    where will proved, 1842

NIXON, George   W-1816   pr 1-p 295, 302
                                                   pr 2-p 7
    wife - Margaret   Lawrence Twp.
    "my own and her heirs"

    Admx - Margaret Nixon

NIXON, John   E-1817   pr 2-p 36, 37, 109, 166
    Admx - Laurana Nixon   Roxbury

NOBLE, H. W.   E-1816   pr 1-p 305-b (2nd of 2 pages
                                                             #305)
    Admr - David Putnam   pr 2-p 20, 32
                                                   Marietta

NOLAND, Philip   W-1842   pr 6-p 310, 359, 361, 435
    wife - Mercy   pr 7-p 305
    4 sons - William, Charles, Barnabas &   Decatur Twp.
                Alexander Noland
    3 daus - Delila Burkley, Sarah Place, and
                Elizabeth Giddings
    step-dau - Morain Engles

    Execx - wife, Mercy Noland

NOLTON   See KNOWLTON

NORMAN, Henry W.   E-1815   pr 8-p 617
    Admr - Aquilla Norman

NORMAN, Joseph   E-1838   pr 5-p 520
    wife & 4 children (no names)   pr 6-p 195
    1st Admr - Elias Pewthers   Roxbury Twp.
    Admr de bonis non - Hiram Gard

*NORTHRUP, Jane   G-1803   pr 1-p 90
            Thomas
            Varnum

    Guardian - Henry Northrup

NOTT, Benjamin   E-1822   pr 2-p 360, 362
    widow - Mary who mar. 2nd _____Morris   pr 3-p 113, 114, 284
    Admr - Amos Wilson   Adams Twp.

NOTT, James   E-1816   pr 1-p 297

NOTT, Simeon   E-1825   pr 3-p 279, 347
    widow - Polly Nott (lives Waterford)   pr 5-p 283, 328 (1836)
    heirs of 3 dec'd sons - Simeon P.,   Roxbury Twp.
            Craven and Tiffin G. Nott
            (details omitted here)
    dau - Philinda, wife of Asa B. Briggs
    sons - Stewart M., Roswell H., Samuel B., of age
            and minor, Harry P. Nott

    Admx - Polly Nott, followed by
    Admr de bonis non - George Bowen (1836)

NULL, Squire   E-1840   pr 6-p 136, 340
    (Squire A.)   pr 8-p 154
    widow, child   Marietta

    Admx - Cynthia Ann Null who married _____
            Farnsworth before estate settled
            in 1848

NULTON, John   E-1850   pr 8-p 510
                                                  pr 9-p 110
    Admr - John Shrader   Watertown Twp.

NYE, Ichabod   E-1842   pr 6-p 405-418
    Admr - A. T. Nye   Marietta Twp.

OAKS, Joel   E-1823   pr 2-p 408, 410
    widow - unnamed   pr 3-p 335
    other heirs - Susan Oaks, Elizabeth Oaks   Belpre Twp.

    Admr - Daniel Oaks

O'BLENESS, Henry   W-1842   pr 6-p 381, 449
    wife - Rachel   pr 7-p 474
    sons - James, Henry & John   Lawrence Twp.
    daus - Phoeby and Eliza
    dau Rachel's children &
    dau Gertrood's children

    Exr - Henry O'Bleness, Jr.

OGLE, James   E-1816   pr 1-p 313
    Admrs - Margaret Ogle &   pr 2-p 28
          Richard Campbell   Salem Twp.

OLIVER, Cyrus   E-1849   pr 8-p 370
    widow - Margaret   pr 9-p 227, 482
    9 minor ch - David, Elizabeth, Giles Eastern,   B-28, 133
       John Western, Christiane, Albert,   Jolly Twp.
       Anne Margarate, Thomas Owings, &
       Henry Oliver
    3 ch of age - Susan Chris, mar to John Chris;
       Hilry Oliver & Nancy Oliver

    Admx - Margaret Oliver

OLIVER, Robert   W-1811   pr 1-p 192
    son - William
    children of son, William - Lancelot, Mary, Minerva,
       Eliza, Elizabeth G., Catherine, Robert
    dau - Anna Quigley
    dau - Christian, wife of William Burnham;
    children of dau. Eleanor, wife of Thomas Lord;
    dau - Margaret Waterman
    heirs of dec'd dau., Mary in New England
    dau, Isabel, wife of James Brown
    son - Robert Oliver

    Exrs - Thomas Lord and James Brown

OLNEY, Coggshall   W-1804   pr 1-p 62, 63, 288
    wife - Sarah   Marietta
    sons - Washington & Discovery
    adopted dau - Jenny unmarried
    dau - Joanne, dec'd late wife of Asa Davis
    dau - Sally, wife of Daniel Davis, Jr., - her children
       Joanna, Edwin Olney and Sophronia Davis

    Exrs - wife, Sarah, Ebenezer Nye & Daniel Davis, Jr.

OLNEY, Eleazer   E-1814   pr 1-p 264, 284, 291
    widow - Susanna   Union Twp.

    Admr - Nathaniel Olney

```
*OLNEY, Mary Matilda              G- 1835              pr 5-p 211
    (dau of Nathaniel Olney)
    Guardian - James M. Booth

OLNEY, Nathaniel                  W-1818              pr 2-p 83, 199
    wife - Mary                                       pr 4-p 500 (1831)
    dau - Matilda Mary, minor                         Union Twp.
    Exrs - widow, Mary Olney & James Whitney

OLNEY, Washington                 E-1826              pr 3-p 531
    children not named                                pr 4-p 155
                                                      Union Twp.
    Admx - Apphia Olney (widow)

OLYPHANT, Ann                     W-1846              pr 7-p 350
    (widow of Newport, R.I.
    where will proved, 1839)
        son - David W. C. Olyphant
        dau - Ann Olyphant
        granddau - Ann V. Olyphant, dau of son, David
    Exr - son, David

O'NEAL, Joseph                    E-1840              pr 6-p 74, 78
    widow                                             Belpre Twp.
    children
    Admr - Benjamin F. Stone

ORRISON, Matthew                  E-1811              pr 1-p 195, 200
    Admr - Nathaniel Hamilton                         Wooster Twp. (early
                                                      name for Watertown Twp.)

OWEN, James                       E-1807              pr 1-p 127, 247
    wife Zuba (also Azuba)                            Adams Twp.

OWEN, (Maj.) Oliver               E-1825              pr 3-p 383, 385
    unsettled partnership witn Thadeus Goodnow        pr 4-p 157
    also, another partnership with John Pope          Watertown Twp.
    Admr - Ebenezer Bowen

OWEN, Ovid F.                     E-1839              pr 5-p 595
    Admr - E. A. Owen                                 pr 6-p 472
                                                      Marietta Twp.
```

```
*PACKARD, Eliza C.          G-1833              pr 5-p 86
         Louisa
         Harriet

    Legatees of Samuel Cobb, late of Boston,
    owner of 1 share in Ohio Company drawn to
    Benjamin Cobb, dec'd, & entitled to 3/16
    of these lands in Washington, Athens &
    Gallia counties, petition to sell land.

    Guardian - Silas Packard of Bridgewater, Mass.


PAIN, John               W-1843              pr 6-p 437, 458, 460
   (also Paine or Payne)                     pr 7-p 268
                                             pr 8-p 466
   wife - Fanny Paine (or Frances)           Waterford Twp.
   son - Charles
   dau - Amy & her 3 children
   grandson - John, oldest son of Charles and
              other childre n of Charles
   son - James and grandson, Joseph, son to James

   Admr - with will annexed - Seth Woodford


PALMER, Ephraim           E-1841              pr 6-p 236, 237
                                             pr 7-p 189
   widow & children got year's support       Wesley Twp.

   Admr - Benjamin F. Palmer


PALMER, Isaac             E-1819              pr 2-p 158, 186
   widow                                     Marietta
   5 minor children, not named

   Admr - Waterman Palmer


PALMER, Jabish F.         E-1840              pr 7-p 121, 130, 389
                                             pr 8-p 602
   widow & heirs                             Watertown Twp.
   Admr - James Dickey


PALMER, William H.        E-1843              pr 6-p 461, 477
                                             pr 8-p 181, 471
   Admr - Boylston Shaw                      Waterford Twp.


PARKER, John              W-1819              pr 2-p 157, 180, 199, 259
   wife - Rachel (mar 2nd, Elisha Ryan, 8-14-1821)  pr 3-p 339
   sons - David, John, James, Joseph         Lawrence Twp.
   daus - Margaret Gardner, Mary Parker,
          & Elizabeth Parker

   Exr - Samuel Dye


PARKER, Richard           E-1838              pr 5-p 576
                                             pr 6-p 189, 350
   widow & 2 small children                  pr 7-p 115
   Admr - John Crawford                      Marietta Twp.
                                             (Harmar)
```

PARMENTIER, John   W-1796   pr 1-p 21, 24
                         (non-cupative Will)   Gallipolis Twp.
     died 16 Sept., 1796

     Admx - Jeanne Francoise Parmentier, widow

PARR, Mary   E-1831   pr 4-p 554
                                                    pr 5-p 503
     Admrs - Stephen Parr & Samuel Parr   Grandview Twp.

PARR, Nathan   W- 1826   pr 3-p 510
                                                    pr 4-p 18, 198
     wife - Mary Parr   Grandview Twp.
     sons - Stephen & Isaac, already provided for
     9 other ch - Samuel, Benjamin, Jesse, Hamilton,
                  Vachel, Rebecca, William Harrison, Catharine
                  & James H. Parr

     Exrs - James Williamson & Mary Parr, wife

PARSONS, Enoch   W-1847   pr 7-p 455
     (of Hartford, Conn. where
      will proved, 1846)
      sons - E. Henry Parsons of Ashtabula, Ohio
             & Samuel H. Parsons
      dau - Mary S. Dickson, wife of James Dickson
      grandson - Thomas E. P. Dickson

      Exr - Samuel H. Parsons

PARSONS, Samuel Holden   E-1789   pr 1-p 1, 3, 13, 30
     (also, Parson)   Marietta

     widow mentioned, not named

     Admr - son, Enoch Parsons
     Admr de bonis non - son, William Walter Parsons
                         apptd, 1794

PATTEN, Richard   E-1801   pr 1-p 48, 49
                                                    Marietta
     Admrs - Ruth Patten & William Patten

PATTERSON, James   E-1795   pr 1-p 17, 51
                                                    Marietta
     Admr - Thomas Stanley

PATTERSON, John   E-1840   pr 6-p 92, 346
     At settlement payments:
        To Joseph Chambers in trust for his daus
        To John Dodge in trust for his children, Patterson
                          & Caroline Dodge
        In hands of admr, & A. O. Patterson, amt in trust
                          for his son, J. E. Patterson

     Admr - A. O. Patterson

```
PATTERSON, Nathaniel          W-1823              pr 2-p 433
    nieces - Esther Patterson, Betsey Seamens,    pr 4-p 34
        and Margaret Wells                        Adams Twp.
    nephew - William Patterson; niece, Margret
        Patterson,; nephew, Samuel Patterson;
        niece, Mary Patterson; nephew,
        James Patterson

    Exr - Truman Ransom

PATTIN, James                 E-1827              pr 4-p 65, 66, 337
    Admr - Wm Pitt Putnam                         Belpre Twp.

PATTON, Mahlon                E-1845              pr 7-p 285, 316
    Admr - Ezekiel Patton                         Roxbury Twp. (or
                                                  Wesley Twp.)

PAYNE, Abram, Sr.             W-1826              pr 3-p 508
    wife - Hannah                                 pr 4-p 13
    daus - Hannah Messinger, Tammy Payne,         Salem Twp.
        Lucinda Whiting, Mary Humphreys
    sons - Abram, Jr. & Rufus Payne
    heirs of dec'd dau - Nancy Stanley
    dau - Lucy Payne
    sons - Norman, William & George Payne

    Exrs - Norman Payne & William Payne

PAYNE, Gabriel                W-1839              pr 5-p 535, 585
    Children:  Abigal Elison, John Payne,         pr 6-p 319
        Samuel Payne, William Payne,              Barlow Twp.
        Hannah Pugh, Joseph Payne and
        Gabriel Payne, Jr.

    Exr - Benjamin F. Palmer

*PAYNE, John                  G-1849              pr 8-p 234
    (insane)

    Guardian - Wm Payne

PAYNE, Norman                 E-1837              pr 5-p 468, 493, 557
    widow & children got allowance               pr 6-p 10

    Admr - Samuel Hussey

PEASE, Hezekiah               W-1791              pr 1-p 7, 9
    (1st U.S. Regt.,      (non-cupative will)
    Capt. Heart's Co.)

    legatee - James Allen of same company

    Admr - Paul Fearing

PECK, Zachariah               E-1822              pr 2-p 275, 386, 403
    Admr - John Gossett, Jr.                      Barlow Twp.
```

```
PEET, Samuel                W-1808          pr 1-p 165, 166, 238
    wife - Mary                             Waterford Twp.
    daus - Olive, Clarissa, Mary Ann
    son - Truman

    Exrs - wife, Mary Peet & William Gray

PEIRCE, Ebenezer            E-1802          pr 1-p 53, 68
    Admr - Levi Allen                       Waterford Twp.

PEIRCE, Stephen             W-1823          pr 2-p 286, 383
    (PIERCE)                                Marietta
    wife - Hannah R. Peirce
    sons - Thomas L. & William (a minor)
           for whom bro. Thomas L. named
           Guardian.

    Exrs - Hannah R. & Thomas L. Peirce

PERKINS, Anthony            E-1813          pr 1-p 239, 308, 309
    widow is Anna who mar. James Dowling, both   pr 2-p 92, 93
        then from Salem Twp., 6 May, 1824   Adams Twp.
    heirs - Edward & Polly Perkins

    Admr - Edward Perkins

PERKINS, Samuel             E-1850          pr 8-p 399, 400, 429
    widow & children (not named)            pr 9-p 386
                                            Salem Twp.
    Admr - David Ward

*PERKINS, Viletta           G-1828          pr 4-p 202
    Dividend of Anthony Perkins Estate is due her.
    Guardian is Anna Dowling, late Anna Perkins,
        widow of Anthony

PERKINS, William            W-1816          pr 1-p 295, 305
    sons - Asa, Ezra, Samuel                pr 2-p 26, 27
    youngest dau - Anna                     Salem Twp.
    another legatee - Elisha Allen

    Exrs - son, Asa Perkins & Elisha Allen

PERRIN, Jesse D.            E-1842          pr 6-p 329, 470
    widow & 1 child got year's support      Adams Twp.

    Admr - Christopher C. Smith

PERRY, Rowland              E-1848          pr 8-p 174
    Admr de bonis non - Samuel B. Robinson  Adams Twp.
    No reference to a previous Admr.
```

PERRY, Thomas   W-1842   pr 6-p 378
    children - Susannah, John & James   pr 7-p 25, 26, 387
    granddaughter - Margaret Perry (dau of Sarah)   Wesley Twp.
    grandson - Andrew Corns

    Admr - Lyman Laflin (after Isaac Perry declined as Exr)

PERVIS, Lydia   W-1853   pr 9-p 347
    lot #551 to M. E. Church   B-64
                                                    Marietta
    Admr - George M. Woodbridge

PETIT, Nicholas   E-1798   pr 1-p 31, 33
    Admr - Stephen Willermy   Gallipolis Twp.

PEWTHER, Elias   W-1840   pr 6-p 84, 124, 130, 131
    wife - Ann F. Pewthers   (verbal)   pr 7-p 489
    children given support but no names   pr 8-p 276
                                                    Roxbury Twp.
    Exr - Joseph Leonard

PFAUTZ, Martin   W-1852   pr 9-p 101, 150, 186
    of Lancaster City, Penna.   B-10
    but visiting Marietta   Marietta Twp.

        sister - Martha A. Pfautz

    Admr - Lorenzo M. Parker

PHELPS, John   E-1823   pr 3-p 58, 60, 554
    Admr - Stephen Hildreth   Marietta

PHILIPS, Ezra   E-1810   pr 1-p 188, 203
    widow - Mary, mr. 2nd _____ Brown *   Waterford Twp.

    Admx - Mary or Polly Brown, late Mary Philips
    *(Note: Mary Philips of Waterford Twp. mar.
            John Brown of Athens County, Ohio, 27 August, 1810)

PHILLIPS, Baylies   W-1839   pr 5-p 538
    sister, Malaney Wadsworth in Newark, Mich.   pr 6-p 55, 192, 351
    bro - Pirce Phillips of Freetown, Assonet, Mass.   Marietta Twp.
    bro - Dean Phillips of Newark, Mich
    sister - Betsey Blossom of Freetown, Assonet, Mass.
        also, several other legatees

    Exr - R(obert) Crawford

PIGNOLET, Joachim   W-1796   pr 1-p 23
    Execx - dau, Jeanne Francoise Pignolet   Gallipolis Twp.
            Parmentier

                            Washington County, Ohio Probate -107-

PITMAN, John K.   W-1826   pr 3-p 502
   (of Providence, R.I. where
   will proved, 1819)

   nephew - William Frost, son of late sister, Susannah
           Frost, dec'd
   to friend, Asa Learned, in trust various properties
           of which rents to sister, Ann Tiffany, then to her
           children & grandchildren, but if none survive
           to sister, Mary Dorrance, widow of Providence

   Exrs - Asa Learned & Mary Dorrance, sister

PITMAN, Saunders   W-1840   pr 6-p 35
   (of Providence, R.I.
   where will probated, 1804)

   wife - Amey
   3 mar. daus - Amey, wife of William Potter
                 Rebecca, wife of James Greene
                 Abigail, wife of Ebenezer Johnson
   grandson - William Frost, son of Susanna Frost, dec'd
   sons - Samuel Pitman & John Hinnicut Pitman
   3 single daus - Mary, Anna & Sarah

   Exrs - wife, Amey & son, John Hinnicut Pitman

PLUMER, Jonathan   E-1808   pr 1-p 112, 179, 202
   (also, Plummer)   Marietta

   Admx - Hannah R. Plummer, wife

PLUMER, William   W-1833   pr 5-p 56, 259, 274
   daus - Fanny Plumer, Catharine Shephard,   Marietta
          Amy Mitchell, Sally Preston, &
          Hetty Tinkham
   sons - John & Rev. William S. Plummer
   also - Timothy Buell & his son, William Plumer Buell
          and Catharine L. Love, formerly Catharine L.
          Kelly, brought up in the family

   Exr - John Cotton, Esq.

POND, Elijah   E-1811   pr 1-p 196
                                                    Wooster (early name
   No property to be appraised   for Watertown Twp.)

POND, Samuel B.   E-1844   pr 7-p 117, 119
                                                    pr 8-p 34
   2 minor ch - get support for 1 year   Barlow Twp.

   Admr - John Clark

```
POOL, Samuel                W-1846          pr 7-p 380, 439, 442
    wife - Mary Eleanor                     pr 8-p 282
    5 sons - John, Thomas R., Samuel, Jonah,    Jolly Twp.
            Richard
    3 daus - Susana Rines, Sarah Elenor, Catherine

    Exr - John Pool (son)


PORTER, Amos                W-1845          pr 7-p 251
    Sons - Simon and Jonathan               Salem Twp.


PORTER, Samuel              E-1826          pr 3-p 380, 382
    No widow mentioned                      pr 4-p 101, 162
    children, all minors - Savanna, Adaline,    Belpre Twp.
            Volunia, Alice and Sally

    Admr - Cummings Porter


PORTER, Simon               W-1843          pr 6-p 441
    wife - Elizabeth                        Salem Twp.
    sons - Simon S., Cyrus F., & Irum Porter
    daus - Louis (e), Mary & Ruth

    Exrs - son, Irum Porter & Ephraim Gould


POWERS, Andres             E-1825          pr 3-p 397
    widow                                   pr 4-p 164
    children                                Waterford Twp.

    Admr - Stephen C. Powers
    Admx - Deborah Powers


PRADEL, Julien             E-1795          pr 1-p 16, 22
    Admr - Nicholas Questel of Gallipolis   Gallipolis Twp.
                                            (now, Gallia Co.)


PRATT, Elisha              E-1824          pr 3-p 135, 144, 308
    widow - Rachel                          pr 4-p 1
    ch of age - Maria & Anna                Adams Twp.
    minors - Eliza, Joshua, Louisa, Seth
            and Lucy Pratt

    Admr - Caleb Emerson


PRIEAU, Nicholas           E-1798          pr 1-p 33, 58
    (PRIOUX)                                Gallipolis Twp. (now in
    Admr - John Peter Romain Bureau         Gallia Co.)


*PRIOR, Evannah            G-1850          pr 8-p 425
    (minor heir of Nathan Prior)            pr 9-p 197

    Guardian - Ezer Thomas
```

PRIOR, Nathan   E-1842   pr 6-p 365, 369
    widow   pr 7-p 499
    children - incl. minor heir Evannah,   pr 8-p 425
            others not ramed   Ludlow Twp.

    Admrs - Richard Scott & Robert Prior

PRIOUX, Timothy   E-1803   pr 1-p 58, 89, 93
    (also PRIOR)

    widow - Barbara
    minor ch - Joseph, Mary and Barbara

    Admr - Isaac Prior

PROCTOR, John M.   E-1845   pr 7-p 236, 238
    widow - Rowena Proctor was guardian of   pr 8-p 148
            heirs (not named)   Barlow Twp.

    Admr - James Lawton

PROCTOR, Nathan   W-1834   pr 5-p 112, 564
                                                       Barlow Twp.
    widow - Abigail
    sons - Henry & John M. Proctor
    daus - Phebe Henry, Lavinah Henry, Polly Gould,
            Nabby Proctor, & Mary R. Houghland
    niece - Elizabeth G. Green

    Exr - John M. Proctor (youngest son)

PRYOR, Samuel   E-1855   pr 9-p 617
    widow - Jemima   B-243, 259, 260
    ch - Polly Ingram, Sally Crow, Nancy Crum,   Barlow Twp.
            Betsey Burton; John Pryor of Iowa and
            grandch - Samuel & Andrew Pryor, ch of Elijah
            Pryor deceased and other ch of sd Elijah
            residing in Iowa

    Admr - Amos Pryor

PURINTON, James   E-1817   pr 2-p 34, 35, 116
    widow - Phoebe   Marietta
    infant dau

    Admr - John Purinton

PUTNAM, (Major) Aaron Waldo   E-1823   pr 2-p 336
                                                       pr 3-p 370
    Admr - William Pitt Putnam   pr 4-p 168
                                                       Belpre Twp.

PUTNAM, Allen   E-1806   pr 1-p 151, 194
    Admx - Anna Putnam   Salem Twp.

PUTNAM, Anna   E-1808   pr 1-p 166, 194
    Admr - Daniel G. Stanley   Fearing Twp.

PUTNAM, Benjamin Perkins   W-1825   pr 3-p 186, 273, 312, 350
    father - David Putnam   pr 4-p 76, 103, 288, 380
    mother   Marietta
    bros & sisters
    widow - not mentioned in will but property
        set off to her (pr 3-p 312)

    Exr - David Putnam

PUTNAM, Betsey   W-1831   pr 4-p 447, 493, 545, 591
    (dau of late Gen'l Rufus Putnam)   Marietta

    surviving sisters - Susanna Burlingame, Martha Tupper
    brothers - William R. & Edwin Putnam
    niece - Elizabeth Tupper
    nephew - Rufus William Howe
    niece - Betsey Porter

    Exr - William R. Putnam (brother)

PUTNAM, (Mrs.) Elizabeth   W-1842   pr 6-p 276, 286, 290, 424
    (widow of Israel Putnam   pr 7-p 362, 363
    of Union)   Union & Marietta Twps.
    3 daus - Helen P. Devol, Elizabeth A. Clarke,
        and Susan C. Putnam
    2 granddaus - Frances Ann & Elizabeth Augusta Chappell,
            children of Laura Ann Chappell, dec'd
    1 son - Lewis J. P. Putnam

    Exrs - William Devol (son-in-law) & Douglas Putnam, nephew

PUTNAM, Ezra   W-1811   pr 1-p 192
    wife - Lucy   Marietta
    daus - Betty Batchelder, Lucy Small &
        Debby Fuller
    granddaus - Betsey & Lucy Putnam

    Execx - Lucy Putnam (wife)

PUTNAM, Israel   W-1812   pr 1-p 200, 259, 261, 272
    (Col. Israel)   pr 4-p 382
    wife - deceased   Belpre Twp.
    3 daus - Polly Mayo, Betsy Craig, Sally Thorniley
    4 sons - Israel, Aaron Waldo, David & George Washington Putnam

    Exrs - sons, Aaron Waldo Putnam & David Putnam

PUTNAM, Israel   W-1824   pr 3-p 121, 131
    wife - Elizabeth   pr 5-p 372
    eldest son - provided for by deed   Union Twp.
    2nd son - Lewis Pope Putnam
    5 daus - Clarina, Helena Penelope, Laura Ann,
        Frances Maria & Elizabeth

    Execx - wife, Elizabeth

PUTNAM, Lucy   W-1818   pr 2-p 85, 140
    daus - Deborough Fuller, Betsy Batchelor   pr 3-p 188
    grandson - Nehemiah Putnam Fuller, Jedediah Marietta
        Fuller
    granddaus - Betsey Fuller, Betsey Putnam & Lucy Putnam
    legatee - Katherine Crawford

    Exr - William Rufus Putnam

PUTNAM, Pascal P.   E-1831   pr 4-p 529, 583
    bro - Lewis J. P. Putnam   pr 5-p 166, 234, 263, 526
    sisters of age - Helen Devol, wife of William Union Twp.
                Devol, Laura Ann Putnam
    2 minor sisters - Elizabeth & Susan

    Admr - Lewis J. P. Putnam (bro)

PUTNAM, Rufus   W-1824   pr 3-p 139, 172, 175
    wife - Persis   pr 4-p 621
    sons - William Rufus & Edwin Putnam   pr 7-p 484
    grandson - Franklin Putnam   Marietta
    daus- Elizabeth Putnam, Persis Howe,
        Susanna Burlingame, Patty Tupper
    3 grandch - surname, BROWNING
    1 grandson - son of Catherine Buckingham

    Exrs - son, William R. Putnam & David Putnam (cousin)

PUTNAM, William Pitt   E-1800   pr 1-p 42, 47, 51
    (also spelled Putman, but this is wrong)

    Admx - Bethiah Putnam
    Admr - William Putnam

QUIFFE, Remy Thiery   E-1796   pr 1-p 20, 25, 28
                                                 Gallipolis Twp. (now in
    Admr - Peter Robert Maquet of Gallipolis   Gallia County)

QUIGLEY, James   E-1845   pr 7-p 226
    widow - Susan Quigley   pr 8-p 29
    minor ch - Henry, Nancy, Lucretia, Columbus & James

    Admr - John D. Chamberlain

QUIGLEY, John   E-1804   pr 1-p 67, 273
    widow - Anne Quigley   Waterford Twp.
    other heirs - Horace, Mary, Sophia, Lucretia,
              Isabella, William, James & John Quigley
    Admr - Robert Oliver

QUIMBY, Daniel   E-1798   pr 1-p 34
    Admr - John Quimby   Marietta

QUIMBY, Daniel   E-1848   pr 8-p 162, 166, 463
    children got allowance for 1 year, but no names   B-2
    Admrs - John Parke & William Quimby   Union Twp.

QUINBY, Deborah   W-1835   pr 5-p 218, 507
    bro-in-law and sister - Underhill & Elizabeth   Fearing Twp.
                  Lynch
    sister - Phebe Quinby
    legatee - John W. L. Brown

    Exr - Underhill Lynch

QUINBY, Phebe   W- 1835   pr 5-p 219, 507
    Legacies to Underhill & Elizabeth Lynch   Fearing Twp.
    and to John W. L. Brown, the son of James & Ziporah Brown

    Exr - Underhill Lynch

RACE, William   W-1841   pr 6-p 250, 283
    wife - Latisha Race   Wesley Twp.
    wife's son - Joseph Wible
    others - David Hart, his wife Jane Amanda Hart
            and her son, William R. Hart
            also, Luition Hart, Charles Bowman,
            Susan Bowman & John Dirk

    Admr with will annexed - Abram W. Goddard; (named
        Exr., David Hart did not serve)

RAINEY, Elias W.   E-1855   pr 9-p 622
   of Noble Co., but had land   B-241, 262
   in Beverly, Washington Co.

    ch of full age - Edward, Elias, William, Winchester,
             also Elizabeth Mummey, wife of James
             Mummey and Mary Boon, wife of
             Samuel Boon
    minors - Zachariah, Jacob & Phebe

    Admrs - Jacob Jordan & William Dougherty

RAMBO, Jacob   W-1803   pr 1-p 57
    wife - Catharine   Waterford Twp.
    one of his sons - Jackson Rambo
    grandson - Jacob Rambo, son of Rebeckah Tenly

RAMSEY, Dr. Robert   E-1847   pr 8-p 42, 471, 473
    widow & 5 children but no names   Beverly in Waterford Twp.
    Admr - Samuel B. Robinson

RANGER, Ephraim   E-1835   pr 5-p 222
    widow & family given allowance   pr 6-p 31
    Admr - Jonas Moore   Marietta Twp.

RANSOM, Charles   W-1791   pr 1-p 6, 8
    1st U. S. Regt.   (non-cupative will) Fort Harmar
    legatee - David Chapman

RANSOM, Theophilus   W-1823   pr 2-p 432
    wife - Sarah   pr 4-p 301
    5 sons - Stephen, Briant, Merritt, Truman Fort Harmar
        & Calvin Noyes Ransom
    dau - Mary Stone
    grandson - Dan Stone
    also, daus - Sally Todd & Mindwell Ransom

    Exr - Truman Ransom (Calvin N. Ransom named but
        did not serve)

RARDEN, William   E-1847   pr 7-p 504, 505, 583
                                               ·pr 8-p 518
    Admr - John N. Rarden   Roxbury Twp.

RARDIN, Henry Jr.   W-1851   pr 8-p 550, 586, 616
    wife - Elinor   B-346
    dau - Lavina and son Albert   Wesley Twp.

    Exr - William Rardin, bro of Berne, Athens Co., Ohio

RARDIN, John   W-1813   pr 1-p 242, 252, 253
    (RARDON)   pr 2-p 68
    wife - Hannah   Wesley Twp.
    sons - William, Henry, David, John Samuel & Moses
    daus - Mary Bartlett, Betsey Rarden & Jane Coleman

    Exrs - son, William Rardin & Joseph Palmer

RATHBUN, Benedict E.   W-1822   pr 2-p 269, 293, 298, 470
                         (non cupative)   pr 3-p 147
    wife - Frances   Belpre Twp.
    bro - John Rathbun
    sisters - Abigail Brown, Rebecca Trumbull
        & Sally Wilcox; also, Sarah Ann Brown
        of Berlin, N.Y. and Job Lawton Riggs of
        Newport, R.I.

    Admr - Amos Dunham

```
RATHBUN, Gideon              W-1838              pr 5-p 510

    wife - Anna
    10 children - Edmun Rathbun, Mercy Frances, David
                  Rathbun, Daniel Rathbun, Elsy Cole,
                  Hiram Rathbun, William Rathbun, Savire
                  Sipy, Elvira Rathbun, John C. Rathbun, a minor

    Execx - Anna Rathbun (wife)


RAY, John McCrush Robert     E-1826              pr 3-p 400
                                                 Wesley Twp.
    Admr - George Ray


REED, Ezekiel                E-1844              pr 7-p 128, 132
                                                 pr 8-p 595
    Admr - Joseph Caywood                        Lawrence Twp.


REED, Joshua                 E-1799              pr 1-p 36, 37, 90
                                                 Salem Twp.
    widow - Mary

    Admx - Mary, widow and
    Admr - Ephraim True


REGNIER, Aurelius R.         E-1848              pr 8-p 221, 230
                                                 pr 9-p 176
    widow - Charlotte                            B-153
    minor ch - Leora & William Miles Regnier     Marietta Twp.

    Admr - Bial Stedman


REGNIER, John B.             E-1822              pr 2-p 250, 284, 398, 401
                                                 pr 3-p 323
    widow - Content                              Aurelius Twp.
    ch of age - Alfred, Hannah, wife of William
                McIntosh, Felix Regnier
    minor ch - Julius, Francis, John D. &
               Aurelius R. Regnier

    Admx - Content Regnier


REGNIER, John D.             E-1849              pr 8-p 331, 340, 341
                                                 Adams Twp.
    widow & minor ch - not named

    Admrs - Maria Regnier & William Devol


*REGNIER, William Miles      G-1853              pr 9-p 176, 508
    (son of Aurelius Regnier, dec'd)             B-9, 153

    Guardian - Charlotte P. Regnier


RENOUARD, Jacques            E-1795              pr 1-p 14
                                                 Gallipolis Twp.
    Admr - John Gilbert Petit, Esq.              (now in Gallia Co.)


REXROAD, Samuel              E-1842              pr 6-p 332, 447
                                                 pr 7-p 69
    widow - Neoma                                Marietta
    Admr - Robert Crawford
```

```
REYNOLDS, John H.              E-1826              pr 3-p 511, 512
                                                   pr 4-p 160
    Admr - Philip Cole                             Warren Twp.

REYNOLDS, Thomas               W-1852              pr 9-p 102, 155
    wife - Sarah                                   B-11, 90, 91, 167
    sons - Daniel H., Abram, Wilson, John, Benedic, Marietta Twp.
        and Thomas
    daus - Emily Larne, Elizabeth Blockley, Phebea
        Knepper, Angelina Reynolds (minor)
        Catherine Reynolds
    also heirs of dec'd dau Rebeckah Thompson

    Exr - William West

RICE, Abel                     E-1795              pr 1-p 18
    Admr - Dr. Jabez True                          Marietta

RICE, Francis                  E-1840              pr 6-p 141, 197
    widow & ch - not named - got allowance         Salem Twp.

    Admr - Peter Rice

RICE, Nathan                   W-1841              pr 6-p 150, 219, 443
    wife - Jemima Rice                             Rainbow Settlement
ch - Zilpha, Thomas, Subrina, Lucy                 Union Twp.

    Admx - Lucy (dau), as named Exrs declined

RICE, Oliver                   W-1836              pr 5-p 331, 361
    nephew, Oliver Rice, son of late bro, Charles Rice Belpre Twp.
    niece - Mary Ames, wife of Cyrus Ames
    niece - Betsey Howe, wife of William T. Howe
    Abigail Rice Brown, granddau of my sister, Ann Brown
    also, several friends, and as residuary legatees,
        Josiah, Asa & William Rice, relation not given

    Exr - William Pitt Putnam

RICE, Thomas                   W-1845              pr 7-p 242
    (of Warwick, R.I., County of
    Kent, where will proved, 1798)

    mentions late wife, Anne Rice, many
    relatives but no children

RICHARDSON, Reuben             E-1850              pr 8-p 541, 543
    widow                                          pr 9-p 360, 367
    children                                       Marietta Twp.

    Admx - Eliza Richardson
```

```
RIGGS, James              W-1815           pr 1-p 281, 290
    wife - Mary                            Grandview Twp.
    sons - Basel, John, Edmund & Samuel
    daus - Maye Sheets, Mary Ridgeway, Jane Williamson
    granddau - Mary Sheets, dau of Martin Sheets

    Exrs - Edmund Riggs (son) &
           Anthony Sheets (son-in-law)

RIGGS, Mary               E-1818           pr 2-p 131, 132, 135
                                           pr 3-p 425
    Admr - Edmund Riggs                    Grandview Twp.

RIGHTMIRE, Robert         E-1818           pr 2-p 107, 109
    widow - Susanna                        pr 4-p 9, 114
                                           Newport Twp.
    Admr - Joseph Barker, Jr.

RILEY, Betsey             W-1846           pr 7-p 303
    sons - John & William                  Marietta
    daus - Mary, wife of George Posey; Susan, wife
           of Ezekiel Hoskinson; Elizabeth, wife of
           Abner McGee
    grandson - J. Hoskinson

    Execx - Elizabeth McGee (dau)

RILEY, James              W-1841           pr 6-p 251
    Execx - wife, Betsey                   Marietta Twp.

ROACH, John               W-1841           pr 6-p 248, 272
    wife - Pamela Roach and her son, Adolphus   Adams Twp.

    Execx - Pamela Roach

ROBBINS, Mary             W-1839           pr 6-p 24
    dau - Melinda Hutson, wife of John Hutson of   Marietta Twp.
          Marietta, - all estate and anything due from
          "my late father, Ebenezer Sweet, of Deerfield Mass."

    Execx - dau, Melinda Hutson

ROBBINS, Reuben           E-1823           pr 2-p 287
    widow - Charity                        pr 4-p 464 (1830) petition
    ch of age (1830) - Stephen, Esther H.,  pr 5-p 161 (1834)
                    & Cyrus                Belpre Twp.
    4 minors - Emeline, Reuben, Elizabeth &
               Levi, had guardian, Levi Robbins in
               Lewis County, N.Y. (1830)

    Admx - Charity Robbins
    Admr - Daniel Goodno
```

```
ROBBINS, Rev. Samuel P.          W-1823              pr 2-p 442, 544
     wife - Patty                                    Marietta
     son - Samuel P. Robbins
     other ch, not named

     Exr - William R. Putnam


ROBINSON, Eli S.                 E-1848              pr 8-p 135, 136, 138
     wife - Mary                                     Salem Twp.
     minor ch - Hansel, Lorane & Willis

     Admr - Morris True


ROBINSON, Jane                   E-1805              pr 1-p 80, 120
     Admr - Samuel Robinson                          Marietta


ROBINSON, William                E-1800              pr 1-p 42, 43
     Admx - Jean Robinson                            Marietta


RODGERS, Joshua                  E-1850              pr 8-p 392, 428
     widow - Adaline                                 pr 9-p 117
     minor child - Catherine                         Watertown Twp.

     Admr - Robert B. Parke


RODGERS, Saunderson H.           E-1847              pr 8-p 3, 41, 553
     wife - (buried at Watertown)                    Lawrence Twp.
     3 children

     Admr - Charles Atkinson


RODGERS, Thomas                  E-1835              pr 5-p 266, 288
     widow & children, not named                     Waterford Twp.

     Admr - William Rodgers


ROE, Thomas                      E-1845              pr 7-p 214, 216, 587
     Admr - Jacob Bridges                            Warren Twp.


ROGERS, Bathsheba                W-1807d             pr 1-p 129, 268
     son - Daniel Dunham                             Belpre Twp.
     dau - Bathsheba Tilton, wife of Joseph Tilton
     grandch - William Wright & Sara Wright

     Exr - Isaac Pierce


ROGERS, Bennett                  E-1801              pr 1-p 45
     (a "transient person")

     Admr - Robert Safford


ROGERS, Joseph                   E-1791              pr 1-p8
     Admr - Ebenezer Sproat, Esq.                    Marietta
```

ROMANS, Amos   E-1853   pr 9-p 505
    widow - Lydia   Wesley Twp.
    infant dau - Mary W.

    Admx - Lydia Romans

ROOD, James   E-1853   pr 9-p 558
    widow - Catherine P.   B-102, 136, 218, 219
    ch - Edna, Charlotte, Edgar   Marietta

    Admr - Richard H. Rood

ROOD, Wine   W-1823   pr 2-p 428
    son - Wine Rood   pr 3-p 75, 195
    daus - Caroline & Matilda Rood   Fearing Twp.

    Exr - Sam'l Andrews (bro-in-law)

ROOT, Sylvanus   E-1825   pr 3-p 387, 390, 446
    Admr - George Bowen   pr 4-p 41
                                                Waterford Twp.

ROOT, William (2nd)   E-1840   pr 6-p 135, 144, 468
    Admr - Andrew Ballard   Decatur Twp.

ROSE, Elisha   E-1841   pr 6-p 262, 267, 429, 482
    widow   pr 7-p 16
                                                Newport Twp.
    Admr - John D. Amlin &
    Admx - Rebecca Rose

ROSS, Andrew   E-1808   pr 1-p 124

ROUSE, Eliza   E-1835   pr 5-p 228, 230, 408
    Admr - Amos R. Harvey   Marietta

ROWLAND, John   W-1850   pr 8-p 514, 538, 583
    sons - William & Robert   Newport Twp.
    daus - Margaret Rowland, Jane Leonard,
        Isabella Rowland
    grandson - Augustus Leonard

    Exr - Robert Rowland
    Execx - Margaret Rowland

RUMBOLD, Henry   E-1826   pr 3-p 514, 516
    widow - Elinor   pr 4-p 202
    Admr - John Crawford   Union Twp.

```
*RUSSELL, Caroline          G-1833              pr 5-p 31
   (dau of John Russell dec'd)

      Guardian - Robert Crawford
      Atty - Arius Nye

RUSSELL, Charles            E-1842              pr 6-p 331, 447
                                                pr 7-p 70, 386
      widow - C. Jane Russell                   Union Twp.
      1 child got support

      Admr - Robert Crawford

RUSSELL, James              E-1824              pr 3-p 171, 363
                                                Belpre Twp.
      Admx - Judea Russell (widow)

RUSSELL, John               E-1829              pr 4-p 329
      9 children - Hiram, William, Charles,     pr 5-p 31, 236
            Jonathan, Lucy Crawford, wife of    Union Twp.
            Robert Crawford; Polly, wife of
            Pardon Cook; Betsey, wife of Tillinghast
            A. Cook; Jane; and Caroline, a minor,
            with gdn Robert Crawford

      Admr - Hiram Russell

*RUSSELL, Julia             G-1853              pr 9-p 446
                                                B-84
      minor child of Charles Russell

      Guardian - William A. Whittlesey

RUTTER, John B.             E-1851              pr 9-p 96, 168, 169, 467
  (RUETER) (RUTER)                              B-31

      widow - Eliza
      ch - Sarah D., Emeline, John
      also John McCune of Keokuk, Iowa

      Admr - Samuel B. Robinson

RYAN, Dennis                E-1845              pr 7-p 167, 212
                                                pr 8-p 44, 45
      Admx - Catharine Ryan (wife)              Watertown Twp.
      Admr - Edward Ryan

RYAN, Edward                E-1847              pr 7-p 510, 533
                                                pr 8-p 43, 44, 240, 522
      Admr - Seth Woodford                      Watertown Twp.

RYAN, James                 W-1824              pr 3-p 123, 134, 178
                                                pr 4-p 372
      wife - Mary                               Marietta Twp.
      Stepdau - Peggy Cotton
      children - not named

      Admr - with will annexed - James Ryan, Jr.
```

SAIFFERT, Michael   E-1818   pr 2-p 121, 124, 192, 217
    Admr - Solomon Dickey   Adams Twp.

SALTONSTALL, John Latimer   W-1821   pr 2-p 213, 222, 226, 562
    sister - Lucretia Hempstead, wife of Giles   pr 5-p 562
            Hemstead   Marietta
    sister - Nancy Lindsley, wife of Rev. S. Lindsley

    Exr - Giles Hempstead (died c 1826, then Admr appt)
    Admr - Giles S. B. Hempstead of Scioto Co., Ohio

SALTONSTALL, Lucretia   W-1823   pr 2-p 389
    daus - Lucretia Hempstead & Nancy Lindly   pr 3-p 125, 303
    grandch - Lucretia Hempstead, Harriet Hempstead,   Marietta
              William Lindley, Lucretia Harriet Lindley

    Admr - Giles Hempstead

SALTONSTALL, Nathaniel   W-1807d   pr 1-p 120, 121, 168
    wife - Lucretia   Marietta
    son - John Latimer Saltonstall
    dau - Polly Saltonstall

    Exrs - son-in-law, Giles Hempstead &
           son, John Latimer Saltonstall

SAMPSON, Crocker   W-1834   pr 5-p 129
    (of Kingston, Mass., (Plymouth Co.)
    where will probated, 1823)

    wife - Rebecca
    son - Benjamin
    daus - Harriet, Rebecca & Lucy

    Exr - Nathaniel Thomas (friend)

SANDFORD, Thomas J. H.   W-1824   pr 3-p 485, 539
    wife - Mary   Marietta
    son - Thomas Harris Sandford (minor)
    bro - Charles Samuel Roberts Sandford of
          Masborough, near Rotheram, County of York, England
    bro-in-law - Philip W. M. Yonge and Harriet Anna Maria, his
                 wife of Winsor Green, England

    Exrs - wife, bro & sister named above, also as gdns
           of son (wife, Mary; bro - Charles S. R. Sanford
           and sister - Harriet Anna Maria Sandford Yonge)

SARGENT, Winthrop   W-1826   pr 3-p 493
    (of Glosterplace near Natches in
    U.S. Mississippi Territory where
    will probated, 1820)

    wife - Mary
    sons - William Fitz Winthrop Sargent &
           George Washington Sargent

    Execx - wife, Mary

SARRASIN, Francis Abel   E-1794   pr 1-p 14, 17, 21
    Admr - John Lewis Violette of Gallipolis   Gallipolis (now in
                                                 Gallia Co., OH)

SAUNDERS, Joseph   E-1849   pr 8-p 376, 378
    widow - Margaret   Roxbury Twp
    minor children - John T., Reuben & Henry

    Admr - David W. Shinn

SCHACTELIN, Jacob   E-1822   pr 2-p 300, 306, 466
                                                pr 3-p 194, 292
    Admr - William Slocomb   Marietta

SCHERER, Jacob   E-1853   pr 9-p 585
  (SHEARER)   P-1855   B-143, 152
    widow - Elizabeth Scherer of Marietta
    minor ch - Catharine of Marietta, John C. &
               Rebecca A. of Madison, Indiana

    Admr de bonis non - Josiah Morgan

SCHIEFFELIN, Jacob   W-1835   pr 5-p 246
    (of New York City where
    will probated, 1835)

    wife - Hannah L.
    sons - Henry H., Richard L., Effingham, Jacob,
           Edward L. & John L. Schieffelin
    dau - Anna Maria S. Ferris

    Exrs - Henry H. & Richard L. Schieffelin (sons)

SCHOONOVER, Henry   E-1842   pr 6-p 353, 354
    widow and children, unnamed   Belpre Twp.

    Admx - Eunice Schoonover

SCHOONOVER, Nicholas   W-1852   pr 9-p 292, 334, 364, 472
    wife - Sarah   B-44, 51, 100
    daus - Elizabeth & Charlotte   Belpre Twp.
    sons - Jacob & Levi
    also minors - Adolphus, Mary, Caroline, Asa; and
                  ch of dec'd son, Henry, in Peoria Co., Ill.

    Admr - Bial Stedman

SCHRIVER, William   E-1842   pr 6-p 399, 400, 477
    widow and children, unnamed   pr 7-p 195, 482
    Admr - David Hendershot   Liberty Twp.

SCHWAB, Peter   E-1828   pr 4-p 241, 243
    widow   Waterford Twp.

    Admr - Daniel Devol

SCOTT, Eliphalet   W-1850   pr 8-p 532
    sons - Mark E., James B.   Aurelius Twp.
    dau - Charlotte Jane Scott

    Exr - Mark E. Scott (son)

SCOTT, Jesse   E-1818   pr 2-p 63, 73
                                                Waterford Twp.

SCOTT, John M.   W-1813   pr 1-p 271, 272
    (of Franklin Co., Ky)

    widow - Kitty Scott
    son - William Henry Harrison Scott
        other children mentioned, not named

    Admx - Kitty Scott
    Admr - Matthew T. Scott

SCOTT, Obadiah   E-1828   pr 4-p 190, 221, 595
    widow - Thankful Scott   pr 5-p 27
    11 children - Celestina Fuller, wife of Nathaniel   Waterford Twp.
                  Fuller of Licking Co., Ohio; Almira
                  Beach, wife of John Beach, Morgan Co., O.;
                  Tracy Scott, Licking Co., Ohio; Obadiah
                  Scott, Waterford; Hannah Scott, Waterford; also,
                  minors - James, Hiram, Rotheus, Adaline,
                  Winchester, and George Scott

    Admr - Sylvester Scott

SEAMENS, Benjamin   W-1812   pr 1-p 201
    (of Natches, Miss. Territory
    but formerly of Adams Twp., Wash. Co., Ohio)

    brothers - Sam, Gilbert, Preserved
    sisters - Susannah Olney, Sabra Sprague, Martha
              Newell & Mary Aitchison
    other legatees - William Seamens; "my namesake Benjamin
                     Seamens"; Benjamin Newell

    Exrs - Samuel Posthelthwait & Joseph Bowen of Miss Territory,
           and Paul Fearing, Ohio

SEAMONS, Gilbert   W-1800   pr 1-p 36
    wife - Martha
    daus - Susanna, Sabra, Martha, Polly
    sons - Samuel, Benjamin, Bennajah, Gilbert
           & Preserved
    grandson - William, son of dau, Sabra

    Admrs - sons, Gilbert & Preserved Seamons

                            Washington County, Ohio Probate -123-

SEARS, Sarah   W-1846   pr 7-p 297
    (widow of Isaac Sears of New York City
    where will was proved, 1806)

        bequests to sister, Rebecca Blagge, wife of John Blagge
            to son-in-law, Thomas Randall;
            to 3 grandsons - Peregrine, James & William Bordieu;
            sons of late dau, Mary Bordieu;
            to granddau. Harriet Artemesia Randall, dau of my
            late dau, Sarah Randall;
            to dau, Hester Smith;
            to dau, Rebecca Sterrett

        Exrs - friends - John Blagge, Gilbert Aspinwall & Martin
                         S. Wilkins, all of New York City

SEELY, Thomas   W-1829   pr 4-p 258
    wife - Margaret   Waterford Twp.
    son - John H. Seely
    6 other children - Abijah Seely; Elizabeth H.
        McIntosh, wife of E. S. McIntosh; Thomas Seely, Jr.,
        Simeon F. Seely, Lucetta A. M. Seely & Sarah S. Dearborn

    Exrs - John H. Seely & Simeon F. Seely

SEEVERS, Abraham   E-1822   pr 2-p 321, 390
                                                           pr 4-p 199
    Admr - Mary Seavers   Fearing Twp.

*SELBY, James C.   G-1851   pr 8-p 601
    minor son of Jeremiah J. Selby   B-146

    Guardian - Dyer Selby, Jr.

SELBY, Jeremiah J.   E-1842   pr 6-p 324, 327, 448
                                                           pr 8-p 238, 601
        child - James C. Selby   Union Twp.

    Admx - Rosanna D. Selby (widow)

SERROT, Peter   E-1796   pr 1-p 21, 26
                                                           Gallipolis (now in
    Admx - Maria Katharine Aveline Serrot, widow   Gallia Co., Ohio)

SHAFFER, John   E-1832   pr 4-p 553, 628
    widow - Polly Shaffer   pr 5-p 73
    minor ch - Peggy, Noble & Wealthy,   Belpre Twp.
               Philip Cooper Shaffer &
               John Shaffer

    Admr - Oliver R. Loring

SHARP, Abraham   E-1822   pr 2-p 299, 300
                                                           pr 4-p 163
    Admr - William Slocomb   Marietta

SHARP, Eliza   E-1844   pr 7-p 93, 94, 483
    Admr - John C. McCoy   Marietta

SHARP, James   W-1818   pr 2-p 84, 117
    wife - Keziah   Marietta
    children - William Thompson Sharp,
           Esther Thompson Sharp, John, Samuel,
           Louisa, James Madison Sharp, George
           & Joseph Sharp.

    Execx - Keziah Sharp

SHARP, John   E-1823   pr 2-p 504, 507
    No heirs listed in any reference   pr 3-p 127, 422, 476
                              Lawrence Twp.
    Admr - James Rayner

SHARP, Peter   W-1825   pr 3-p 190, 365
    wife - Mary   pr 4-p 118
    only dau - Eliza   Wesley Twp.

    Exr - Jabish F. Palmer

SHAW, Augustus Warner   E-1851   pr 8-p 586, 611, 613
    widow - Lydia M. Shaw   pr 9-p 444
    4 minor ch - Benjamin Dana Shaw, Rutheus   B-66, 67, 203
           Warner Shaw, Panthea Georgiana Shaw
           & Augusta Carr Shaw

    Admr - Dudley S. Nye

SHEETS, Anthony   W-1835   pr 5-p 180, 224, 409
    wife - Maxy Sheets   Grandview Twp.
    daus - Melinda & Axius Sheets; Nancy, wife of
           Benjamin Fort; Polly, wife of John Talbot;
           and Ruth Sheets, wife of Isaac Par
    sons - Martin & Henry Sheets
    also - Julian Sims

    Execx - Maxy Sheets

SHEETS, John   E-1824   pr 3-p 258, 348, 442, 529
    Admr - Anthony Sheets   Grandview Twp.

SHEETS, John C.   E-1847   pr 7-p 506, 508
                              pr 8-p 196
    Admr - Anthony Sheets   Grandview Twp.

SHEETS, Martin   W-1845   pr 7-p 257, 278
    wife - Sally   pr 8-p 192
    sons - John C., Henry J., William,   Grandview Twp.
           Matthias & Anthony
    daus - Mary Kigar, Nancy Dye, Prissilla Dye, Elizabeth J. Dye

    Exr - Daniel Dye

SHEETS, Sarah   E-1845   pr 7-p 279

At settlement equal shares to Anthony Sheets,   pr 8-p 192
H. J. Sheets, Robert Dye, Matthias Sheets, David   Grandview Twp.
Dye, William Sheets, John Sheets & Daniel Dye

Exr - Daniel Dye

SHELDON, Jeremiah   E-1828   pr 4-p 181, 226, 388, 428

widow - Olive   Warren Twp.
minor children - Jeremiah, Fayette, & William
                 Washington Sheldon, under
                 age of 14 in 1830

Admrs - Israel Sheldon & Olive Sheldon

SHEPARD, Anna   E-1823   pr 3-p 34
                                           Marietta

SHEPARD, Enoch   W-1821   pr 2-p 220, 241, 469

wife - Margaret   Marietta
ch of 1st wife, Esther - Enoch, Anna, Rhoda, Daniel,
     Lorana, Luther, Huldah & Calvin Shepard
ch of present wife - Silas M. & Elizabeth G. Shepard

Exr - Silas M. Shepard

SHEPARD, John   E-1844   pr 7-p 61, 143

Admr - Enoch Davis

SHEPHERD, John   E-1847   pr 7-p 575, 577
                                           pr 8-p 43, 239
Admr - George Shepherd   Jolly Twp.

SHEPHERD, Louman   E-1848   pr 8-p 141, 174,

widow   pr 9-p 57
2 ch under 16 (no names)   B-96
                                           Adams Twp. (Lowell)
Admr - Caleb Emerson; 2nd Admr - Melvin Clarke

SHERLOCK, John   E-1847   pr 7-p 582

heirs - Miss A. H. Sherlock   pr 8-p 9, 62, 453
       Mrs. Ann Hoctor   Harmar

Admr - John Burks (Burke)
Admx - Honora Sherlock

SHERMAN, Timothy   E-1827   pr 4-p 145, 147, 538
    ch - Heman Sherman, res. unknown; Lyman   pr 5-p 36
        Sherman of Sandusky, Marion Co., Ohio; Electa Waterford Twp.
        Sherman Loomis, wife of Daniel Loomis of
        Rochester, N.Y.; Olive Sherman Wood, of Dresden,
        Muskingum Co., Ohio; Curtis Sherman of Tuppers Plains,
        Meigs County, Ohio; Abel Sherman, of Waterford, Wash.
        Co., Ohio; Wakeman Sherman, of Morgan Co., Ohio and
        Uri Sherman of Waterford Twp., Wash Co., Ohio

    Admr - Heman Sherman; then
    Admr de bonis non - Henry Stull

SHIPMAN, Frederick   E-1839   pr 6-p 63, 93
    widow and children - not named   pr 7-p 148
                                 pr 8-p 147, 357
    Admr - Samuel Shipman (bro)   Marietta

SHIPMAN, Joseph C.   E-1833   pr 5-p 70
    (late of Virginia)

    Admr - Samuel Shipman

SHIPMAN, Joshua   E-1823   pr 3-p 44, 182
    (for 9 heirs of Joshua, see petition of   pr 4-p 204
    admr of Joshua, Jr. - pr 5-p 43)   Marietta

    Admr - William H. Shipman (son)

SHIPMAN, Joshua, Jr.   E-1831   pr 4-p 519
    (of Wheeling, Va.)   pr 5-p 43 (petition),
                                  also, 76
    widow - Eunice
    1 minor ch - Julia
    petition gives his bros & sisters, heirs with
    him of estate of father, Joshua, Sr.

    Admr - William Slocomb

*SHIPMAN, Susan E.   G-1835   pr 5-p 47. 232
        George C.
        Ann   Children of William H. Shipman, dec'd
        William H.

    Reference to their grandfather, Joshua Shipman's estate
    and to that of Joseph C. Shipman (their uncle)

    Guardian - Samuel Shipman (uncle)

SHIPMAN, William H.   E-1831   pr 4-p 521
    (of Wheeling, Va. where he died, April, 1829)   pr 5-p 47, 71, 232

    widow - Mary Ann Shipman
    4 minor children - Susan, George, Ann E. &
                    William H.

    1st Admr in Va., not given;
    Admr de bonis non - William Slocomb

```
SHORT, Elijah                    E-1846          pr 7-p 378, 395, 405, 503
    wife - Julia A. Short                        Adams Twp.
    minor ch - Mary, Turner, Waterman & Richard Short
    Admr - S. B. Robinson

SHUTTLESWORTH, Joshua            W-1843          pr 6-p 462
    wife - Nancy                                 Wesley Twp.
    minor ch - (unnamed)
    Exr - Walter Kidwell of Barlow

SIMPSON, William                 E-1790          pr 1-p 5
    a soldier in Heart's Company
    Admr - Capt. Jonathan Heart

SIMS, Thomas                     E-1821          pr 2-p 229
                                                 Newport Twp.

SINCLAIR, Martin                 E-1851          pr 9-p 7, 78, 579
    widow - Naomi J. Sinclair                    B-209
    ch under 15 - William M., Jesse P. & Charles A.   Marietta
    ch of full age - Mary M. and Sarah J.
    Admx - Naomi Jane Sinclair

SIRIG, George                    W-1849          pr 8-p 372
    wife - Louisa                                Independence Twp.
    sons - Augustus & Henry
    Exr declined - no admr appt

SKINNER, Henry                   E-1845          pr 7-p 234, 235
    widow - Charity Skinner                      pr 8-p 31
    Admr - Samuel B. Robinson                    Waterford Twp.

SKINNER, William                 W-1841          pr 6-p 169, 284, 296, 303
    wife - Mary                                  pr 7-p 366
    dau - Sarah C. Ward                          Marietta Twp. (Point Harmar)
    sons - David C., William P. & Charles S. Skinner
    Exr - David C. Skinner (son)

SLATER, Ellis                    E-1855          pr 9-p 611
    Heirs - David L., James W.                   B-268, 270, 271
            Mary L. and Emma J. Slater           Beverly
    Admr - David P. Slater

SMITH, Aaron                     E-1823          pr 2-p 290
                                                 pr 3-p 191, 551
    Admr - John Merrill                          Marietta
```

SMITH, George   E-1833   pr 5-p 9, 125
    Admr - Sampson Cole   Marietta

SMITH, Col. Henry   E-1820   pr 2-p 211
    (of Providence, R.I.)   pr 3-p 468
    petition to sell Ohio land to pay
    debts through attorney Benjamin P. Putnam
    Admx & widow - Abby C. Smith

SMITH, Hester   W-1847   pr 7-p 457
    (widow of Paschal Nelson Smith of N.Y. City
    but will proved in New Haven, Conn, 1823)
    heirs - nephews & nieces
    Exrs - John Aspinwall (nephew) &
           George W. Strong

SMITH, Hiram   E-1853   pr 9-p 418, 420, 462
    widow - Caroline   B-73
    minor ch - Ethelinda & Elvira   Grandview
    Admr - Adolphus A. Smith

SMITH, James   E-1801   pr 1-p 42, 43, 44, 65, 89
    wife - Priscilla   Adams Twp.
    1 child - not named
    Admx - Priscilla Smith, widow, later wife of
           Ebenezer Culver

SMITH, John C.   E-1852   pr 9-p 216, 356
    (SCHMIDT)   B-43
    widow - Mary E.   Marietta
    minor ch - Caroline, Amelia, John, Peter
               and unnamed infant
    Admx - Mary E. Smith

SMITH, Michael   W-1845   pr 7-p 247
    wife - Preselle
    children - Hannah, Jane, Emly & Daniel Smith

SMITH, Nathan   E-1800   pr 1-p 37, 39, 41
    Admr - Simeon Deming   Marietta

SMITH, Nathaniel   W-1817   pr 2-p 18, 55, 189
    widow - Jemima Smith   Marietta
    2 ch - Benjamin Franklin Smith &
           Nathaniel Augustus Smith
    Execx - wife - Jemima
    Exr - Dr. John B. Regnier

                    Washington County, Ohio Probate -129-

```
SMITH, Pascal Nelson              W-1850          pr 8-p 510
   (of New York City where                        pr 9-p 67
   will certified, 1835)

      wife - Hester
      4 ch - Harriet, Augusta, William Temple
            and Georgiana (all under 21)

      Execx - Hester Smith
      Exrs - Benjamin Strong (nephew) &
            John Aspinwall (nephew)


SMITH, Patrick                    E-1849          pr 8-p 261, 271, 461
   Admr - Dudley S. Nye                           Marietta Twp.


SMITH, Samuel                     E-1824          pr 3-p 181, 304
      widow - Jamima C. Smith                     Marietta Twp.
      heirs - not named

      Admx - Jamima C. Smith


SMITH, Sumner                     E-1823          pr 2-p 391, 393
      Admr - Nahum Bent                           Belpre Twp.


SMITH, William                    E-1851          pr 8-p 585, 615
      sons - Elijah G., Samuel R., William        pr 9-p 214, 404
      heirs of son John - Hannah, wife of Jefferson   B-68
         Carroll of Gallia Co.; Clarinda, wife of     Harmar
         John Hearn of Gallia Co.
      daus - Mary, wife of Richard Patton, Wash. Co.;
         Hulda, wife of John Test, Wash. Co.; Sarah W.,
         wife of John Newton of Lawrence Co.

      Admr - Elijah G. Smith


SNODGRASS, Beniah                 E-1849          pr 8-p 270, 297, 331
      widow - July Ann Snodgrass                  Lawrence Twp.
      minor ch - Washington, Mary, Anna
               William & an unnamed infant

      Admr - Alexander Clark


SOLOMON, Isaac                    W-1848          pr 8-p 103
      daus - Catherine, Margaret
      grandson - Isaac Wicter Solomon


SOUTHMAYD, Samuel                 W-1838          pr 5-p 463
   (of Watertown, Conn., Litchfield Co.
   where will proved, 1810)

      wife - Dorcas
      heirs of dau,  Milisant Scoville;
      ch - Philamela Fenn; Samuel W. Southmayd;
         Dorcas Dutton; & Alma Deforest

      Exrs - Samuel W. Southmayd & Benjamin Deforest
```

SPACHT, Anthony   E-1803   pr 1-p 58
    Admr - Jacob Spacht, eldest son   Belpre Twp.

SPEARS, Ebenezer   W-1835   pr 5-p 182, 225, 257, 445
    wife - Polly Spears   Salem Twp.
    ch - Daniel, Ebenezer, Susannah, Polly &
        Roxena Spears

    Exr - son-in-law - Charles Spears

SPRAGUE, Anthony W.   E-1849   pr 8-p 318, 321, 333, 570
    widow   Adams Twp.
    children

    Admr - Augustus W. Sprague

*SPRAGUE, Benjamin O.   G-1845   pr 7-p 313

    now age 21 years - settlement by

    Guardian - S. M. Devol

SPRAGUE, Jonathan   W-1840   pr 6-p 42, 93, 133
    widow - Hannah   pr 7-p 67
    sons - Elijah, Seamons, Benjamin, A. W. &
        Jonathan Sprague
    son - Joshua Sprague's heirs, i.e. - J. G., Cynthia M.,
        and Oliver P. Sprague

    Exr - Anthony Wayne Sprague

SPRAGUE, Joshua   E-1824   pr 3-p 66
    See also Guardian accts. for heirs,   pr 4-p 127
    Oliver P., Cynthia M., & John G. Sprague Adams Twp.

    Admx - Phebe G. Sprague, widow, was Phebe G. Ross
        at settlement

SPRAGUE, Nehemiah   E-1820   pr 2-p 187, 188
    Admr - Jonathan Sprague   Adams Twp.

*SPRAGUE, Oliver P.   G-1830   pr 4-p 342
        Cynthia M.   pr 5-p 373
        John G.

    Children of Joshua Sprague, dec'd

    Guardian - John Brown

*SPRAGUE, Oliver P.   G-1851   pr 8-p 565
    insane heir of Joshua Sprague   pr 9-p 174, 232
                               B-34
    Guardian - Jonathan Sprague

```
*SPRAGUE, Seamons                G-1845              pr 7-p 313
    now age 21 years - settlement by               Adams Twp.
    Guardian - S. M. Devol

SPRAGUE, William                 E-1826              pr 4-p 19, 21, 22, 23, 295
    widow                                           Adams Twp.
    Admx - Experience Sprague was Experience
         Dodge at settlement

SPRINGER, Jacob                  W-1830              pr 4-p 358, 453
    wife - Catherine                                pr 5-p 395
    sons - Humphrey H., Jacob, John, Garrett        Warren
         and Peter Springer
    daus - Susannah Misner & Jane Morris
    Exr - Jesse Loring

SPRINGER, Peleg                  W-1829              pr 4-p 231, 265
    wife - Sarah                                    Watertown Twp.
    sons - Joseph, Clark, Harris, Albert
    daus - Lucy Hudson, Betsey Dodge
    Execx - Sarah Springer, wife

SPROAT, Ebenezer (Col.)          W-1805              pr 1-p 74, 75, 94, 108, 110
    wife - Katherine                                Marietta
    dau - Sarah
    Execx - Katherine Sproat, wife

SQUIRES, Justice                 W-1791              pr 1-p 6, 9
                       (non-cupative will)          Fort Harmar
    A member of 1st U.S. Regt.
    His only legatee is John Nelson
    Admr - Paul Fearing

STACEY, William                  E-1802              pr 1-p 51
    Admrs - sons - William & Gideon Stacey          Marietta

STANBERY, Jonas                  W-1843              pr 7-p 6
    of Zanesville, Ohio (Muskingum
    Co.,) where will proved, 1840
    wife - Ann Lucy
    sons - Harvey, Henry, Edward, Charles, Howard & Jonas
    dau - Ann Lucy Peirce
    step dau - Eliza Flanner
    Exrs - sons - Henry & Howard Stanbery
```

STANLEY, Amzi   E-1823   pr 3-p 53, 55
    Admr - Joseph Barker, Jr.   pr 4-p 83
                                                   Marietta

STANLEY, Daniel G.   W-1853   pr 9-p 334, 351, 353,
    sons - James, Thomas & Lot Putnam Stanley   360, 599
    dau - Rosella Merriam (p 599)   B-65, 266
    heirs of deceased dau, Mrs. Babson (p 599)   Fearing Twp.
    adopted son - George Washington Putnam
    adopted dau - Martha W. Cotteral

    Exr - bro, James Stanley

STANLEY, Eliza   E-1823   pr 3-p 65, 258
    Admr - Lucius Cross   pr 5-p 153
                                                   Marietta

STANLEY, Thomas   W-1817   pr 2-p 1
    wife - Mixenda   Salem Twp.
    5 sons - Daniel Griswold Stanley, Thomas Ford
             Stanley, Francis Rowlandson Stanley,
             James Stanley & George Stanley
    8 daus - Anne, Betsey, Lucy, Clarecy, Cynthia,
             Sarah, Mary & Mixenda

    Execx - wife, Mixenda Stanley &
    Exr - son, Daniel G. Stanley

STANLEY, Timothy   W-1819   pr 2-p 105
    wife - Abigail   pr 5-p 154, 369
    son - Timothy Robbins Stanley   pr 6-p 154
    daus - Abigail, Thirza, Eliza; Lydia   Marietta Twp.
           Newell, Mary Kellog, Julia Caroline Stanley
           and Electa Wells

    Execx - wife, Abigail, then
    Admr de bonis non - Lucius Cross, appt.

STANTON, Joseph   E-1843   pr 6-p 430, 433
    widow & family got year's support.   pr 8-p 142
                                                   pr 9-p 61
    Admr - Jacob Bridges   Warren Twp.

STARLIN, Simon   E-1821   pr 2-p 210, 248
    widow   pr 3-p 116
    son - Simon Starlin, Jr.   Wooster Twp. (former name
                                                   for Watertown Twp.)
    Admx - Elizabeth Starlin

STEARNS, Amos   W-1813   pr 1-p 232, 240
    (Sterne)   Belpre Twp.

    father & mother - Elias & Sarah Stearns
    brother - Rufus Stearns

    Exrs - Aaron W. Putnam and brother,
           Asa Stearns

                    Washington County, Ohio Probate -133-

STEVENS, Abraham   W-1828   pr 4-p 210, 244
                                                    pr 5-p 138
    wife - Rachel   Waterford Twp.
    sons - Samuel, John, David, James
    grand ch - children of dec'd oldest dau,
                Delila Perry, late wife of John Perry;
                ch - of 2nd dau, Sally Williams, wife of
                Joseph Williams;
                ch - of Amarilla Chapman, wife of Nathaniel
                Chapman

    Exrs - Samuel & John Stevens (sons)

STEVENS, Peter B.   W-1839   pr 5-p 571
                                                    pr 6-p 67, 392
    widow - not named   pr 7-p 262
    only dau - Sarah Ann Catherine Stevens, and   Belpre Twp.
                if she dies, to cousins - Peter
                Stevens of N.Y. State; Ben Snider
                Stephens & Ephraim Stephens

    Exr - Cummings Porter

    Extra note--Widow is probably Maria Ball, as there is
    a marriage - in Washington County - of Peter B. Stephens
    to Maria Ball of Decatur (he being from Belpre Twp.)
    10 Sept., 1835; also, an earlier one: Peter B. Stephens
    to Abigail Coggeshall 16 Sept. 1822 in Washington County, Ohio

STEWART, Archibald   W-1843   pr 7-p 8
    (of Providence, R.I.
     where will proved, 1805)

    wife - Austis
    son - Charles
    dau - Jane Stewart Lawrence, wife of Walter Lawrence
    legatee - Peggy Reed
    sons of bro Richard Stewart in Ireland;
    sons of sister, Rose Thompson's 2 daus in Ireland
    stepson - William Hutton

    Exrs - friends, Nathan Waterman & John Dorrance

STEWART, John   E-1822   pr 2-p 371, 372
                                                    Warren Twp.
    Admx - Susanna Stewart

STILL, Daniel   E-1853   pr 9-p 495
                                                    B-120
    widow - Lavina
    son - Daniel (infant)

    Admr - John Still

STILLE, Ebenezer   W-1821   pr 2-p 205, 218
    wife - Esther   Salem Twp.
    children - not named

    Exr - Simon Porter

STILLWELL, Elias   W-1837   pr 5-p 416
(of New Haven, Conn. where will
probated, 1824)

    widow - Mary
    others, relation not given - Hezekiah Howe, Sally Townsend,
    wife of Amos Townsend; Hannah Collis, wife of Solomon Collis;
    Ebenezer Howe, eldest son of Hezekiah Howe; Elias Stillwell
    Townsend, eldest son of Sally Townsend; Hannah Stillwell Collis,
    eldest dau of Hannah Collis

    Admr - Roger S. Skinner

    Note -- Those named in will are likely a widowed bro-in-law,
            2 married sisters, 2 nephews & a niece.

STONE, Benjamin F.   E-1824   pr 3-p 253
                                                     pr 5-p 162
    Allowance for family's support but no names   Belpre Twp.

    Admr - John Stone

STONE, Clarissa   W-1846   pr 7-p 344, 373, 374, 378
                                                     pr 8-p 152
    4 nephews - Stephen Stone, Dan H. Stone,   Marietta
                Charles Stone, Sherlock Stone
    2 sisters - Catherine Stone & Mary Stone

    Exr - Dan H. Stone

*STONE, Dan   G-1828   pr 4-p 227

    Guardian - John Russell

STONE, Israel   E-1808   pr 1-p 168, 175, 179, 184
                                                     pr 2-p 25
    Heirs are: Sardine Stone, B. F. Stone, Matilda   Adams Twp.
    Smith, Jasper Stone, John Dodge, Truman
    Guthrie for himself & as guardian of Harriet
    H. Stone; Ezra Hoyt; A. Stone for himself and
    as gdn. for C. C. Stone as shown in signatures
    of petition (pr 1-p 184)

    Admr - Sardine Stone

STONE, Jasper   W-1830   pr 4-p 407, 419, 497, 567
                                                     pr 5-p 127, 134
    3 daus - Amanda, Collina & Vesta Stone   Union Twp.
    son - Jasper Converse Stone
    bounden apprentice - Solomon Hallet

    Exr - bro - Benjamin Franklin Stone

STONE, Jonathan   E-1801   pr 1-p 44, 51, 67
     Admx - Susanna Stone (widow)   Belpre Twp.
     Admr - Benjamin Franklin Stone (son)

*STORRS, William H.   G-1853   pr 9-p 380
     Arabella   B-69, 72

        minor ch of William Storrs dec'd, late of
          marietta and of Sophronia A. Storrs now
          Mrs. Russell Harris

        Guardian - George M. Woodbridge

 STORY, Andrew   E-1826   pr 3-p 392
     widow   Waterford Twp.

*STORY, Andrew   G-1850   pr 8-p 411, 419, 603
     Silas
     William   heirs of Michael Story, dec'd
     David

        pr 8-p 411 & 419 - accts. of guardian,
                           Charles Story
        pr 8-p 603 (1851) settlement by Silas Brown, Admr
                           of Charles Story, dec'd

 STORY, Betsey   E-1848   pr 8-p 210, 212, 464, 603

        1851 Settlement shows legacies of
        1 share to Silas Brown, admr. of Charles Story, dec'd;
        1 share divided into 6 parts (5Browns & wife of
            Charles G. Culver);
        1 share divided into 5 parts, heirs of Michael Story;
        1 share to Samuel Story's heirs and
        1 share to Polly Powers

        Admr - Charles G. Culver

 STORY, Charles   E-1849   pr 8-p 299, 304, 330, 592
     widow   Waterford Twp.

     Admr - Silas Brown

 STORY, Daniel   E-1805   pr 1-p 70, 79, 93, 96, 107,
     Admr - William Burnham of Marietta   167, 173, 176, 177
                                                 Marietta Twp.

 STORY, Michael   E-1842   pr 6-p 278, 321, 447
                                                 pr 7-p 153, 265
        At settlement, 1/3 to Relief B. Brigham, so   pr 8-p 603
        she is probably the widow, remarried; 2/3   Waterford Twp.
         to children - Andrew, Silas, William, David

        Admr - John D. Chamberlain

        Note - probable marriage of widow (v 2, p 54)
               C. C. Brigham of Marietta to Relief B. Story of
               Waterford, 1 Sept., 1842 by Samuel McCollum

```
STULL, Perez                    E-1823              pr 2-p 500
                                                    pr 3-p 96
        Admx - Frances Stull                        pr 4-p 50
                                                    Waterford Twp.

STULL, Wickam                   E-1829              pr 4-p 264
                                                    Waterford Twp.

STURGIS, Russell                W-1831              pr 4-p 524
    (of Boston, Mass. where
    will probated, 1826)

    wife - Elizabeth
    sons - Nathaniel Russell Sturgis,  James Perkins Sturgis,
        George Washington Sturgis
    daus - Sarah Paine Pope, Elizabeth Sturgis, Ann Cushing
        Sturgis
    late bro - Capt. Thomas Sturgis, his widow, Elizabeth
        & 3 daus

    Execx - wife - Elizabeth Sturgis

TAGUE, Edward                   W-1850              pr 8-p 513

    wife
    3 daus - one named Mary
    2 sons

    Exrs - Peter Tague & Patrick Nugent of
        Hampton Twp., Perry County, Ohio

TALBOT, Edward                  E-1852              pr 9-p 253, 271, 294, 300
    widow - Catherine                               B-43, 45, 47
    4 ch of full age, living in Plymouth, Wash. Co. Wesley Twp.
        Aquila D., Henry & John E. Talbot; Amanda F
        Johnson, wife of William S. Johnson
    2 ch of full age living in Martinsville, Belmont Co.
        Susan Brown, wife of Henry Brown; Ann G. Riggle,
        wife of Henry Riggle
    1 minor ch - Ralph

    Admr - Aquila Talbot

TAYLOR, John                    W-1836              pr 5-p 317, 435, 528
    (late of England but now of                     Union Twp.
    Union Twp.)

    Execx - sister, Margaret Taylor

TAYLOR, Margaret                E-1845              pr 7-p 200, 202
        Admr - John Crawford                        pr 8-p 30
```

TAYLOR, Peter   W-1833   pr 5-p 92, 120, 122, 497
   wife - Margaret   Watertown Twp.
   children (not named)

   Exr - Joseph Palmer, widow relinquished

TAYLOR, Robert   E-1801   pr 1-p 48, 50
   Admr - William Taylor   Marietta

TAYLOR, William   W-1823   pr 2-p 429
   sisters - Fanny Taylor, Jane Miller,   pr 3-p 51, 53, 285
          Catherine Miner & Maria Guitteau   Marietta

   Exr - John Miller

TEMPLETON, George   E-1850   pr 8-p 489, 505, 509
                                          pr 9-p 519
   widow - Nancy Templeton   B-54, 139, 147
   heirs - Eliza Bartmess, wife of Jacob Bartmess;   Lawrence Twp.
      Joseph Templeton; Samuel Templeton;
      James Templeton; Letty M. Templeton;
      Margaret Atkinson, wife of James Atkinson,
      of full age; ch of William Templeton, dec'd;
      ch of Jane Atkinson, dec'd, residing in Wash.
      Co., Ohio; Mary Snodgrass, wife of Eli Snodgrass;
      and Robert Templeton of Iowa

   Admr - Richard Scott

TEMPLETON, William   E-1840   pr 6-p 185
   Admx - Anna H. Templeton (1st ref)   pr 8-p 101
   Admr de bonis non - John Crawford (1847)   Lawrence Twp.

THOMAS, Jacob   E-1850   pr 8-p 396, 428
   widow - Elizabeth   pr 9-p 410, 464
   minor ch - Isaac, John L., Benjamin F.,
       Samuel R., Nancy J. & James M. Templeton

   Admr - Dr. Richard Scott

THOMAS, Jesse   E-1842   pr 6-p 373, 375
   widow - Rebecca   pr 8-p 290

   Admr - John H. Livesay (Livezy)

THOMAS, Jonathan   E-1823   pr 3-p 63, 192
   Admr - Isaac Barstow, then   pr 4-p 106
   Admr de bonis non - Enoch Thomas   Warren Twp.

THOMAS, Peter Thomas   E-1796   pr 1-p 22, 27
   Admr - Simon Subbil, a creditor   Gallipolis Twp. (now in
                                           Gallia Co., Ohio)

THOMPSON, Arthur   E-1825   pr 3-p 346
    Widow   Marietta

    Admx - Elizabeth Thompson (probably the widow)

THOMPSON, James   W-1837   pr 5-p 423
    (of Baltimore, MD. where
    will probated, 1837)

    niece - Sarah Jane Little
    other heirs - cousins or nephews - (?) - 4 bros., sons of
        James St. Moore of Antrim, Ireland - William, John, James
        and one other
    cousin - Mary Moore of Wheeling, Va.
    sister - Mary Thompson of Baltimore

    Exrs - Sarah Jane Little & George Law of Baltimore
        and David Barber of Ohio

THOMPSON, Joseph   E-1801   pr 1-p 46

    Admr - Robert Oliver, Esq.

THORNILEY, Caleb   E-1810   pr 1-p 188, 189
    (also Thornley & Thornily)   Marietta Twp.

    Admr - son - William Thorniley

THORNILEY, Caleb   E-1823   pr 3-p 98, 289
    Admr - John Thorniley   Marietta Twp.

THORNILEY, Caleb W.   E-1828   pr 4-p 252, 546
    widow - Tabitha   Marietta Twp.
    minor ch - William Irwin, Cornelia Ann
            & John C. Thorniley

    Admx - Tabitha Thorniley, widow

THORNILEY, John   W-1844   pr 7-p 107, 123
    wife - Mary   pr 8-p 26
    ch - William; Mary Ann Howe, wife of Aaron   pr 9-p 484
        Howe; Thomas C.; Caleb S.; James;   B-122
        Adaline V.; Elizabeth; John. By the   Marietta Twp.
        settlement, Thomas C. & John are deceased
        & Elizabeth living in Pike Co., Missouri

    Exrs - Mary Thorniley, wife & son, William Thorniley

THORNILEY, Sally   E-1819   pr 2-p 110, 111, 175, 253
    An acct. between her heirs and William   265, 387
    R. Putnam, her guardian   pr 4-p 382
                                                    Marietta
    Admr - David Putnam

THORNILEY, William   E-1827   pr 4-p 112, 150, 246
                                                        404, 455
    widow - Elizabeth   Marietta
    minor ch - William & Thomas
    other heirs - dau Augusta, wife of James Berwick;
    4 minor ch of dec'd son, Caleb W. Thorniley, namely -
    William Irvin, Cornelia,Ann & John, listed in July,
    1829 petition (404)

    Admr - Philip V. Thorniley

THORNILEY, William J.   E-1853   pr 9-p 463, 509
                                                     B-79, 85, 86, 98, 119, 121
    widow - Esther A.   Marietta
    ch of full age - Samuel S. & Elizabeth Thorniley
    minors - Augusta B., wife of George Harness;
              Eliza D. & Laura J. Thorniley

    Admr - Samuel S. Thorniley & Andrew G. Batelle

THORNTON, Marcy   W-1834   pr 5-p 116
   (of Warwick, R.I., Co. of Kent, where
   will probated, 1833)

    widow - of Christopher Thornton, dec'd

    legatees - Marcy Aborn, wife of Joseph Aborn;
               Phebe Thornton, widow of late William Thornton;
               Sally Aborn, dau of late Lowry Aborn;
               Sarah Desire Aborn, dau of the late John Anthony Aborn;
               Henrietta Aborn, dau of Thomas Aborn;
               Phebe Harris, wife of Daniel Harris

    Exr - friend, Joseph Aborn of Cranston

THROOP, Zebulon   E-1790   pr 1-p 10, 12
    Admr - Robert Oliver, Esq.   Marietta

TICE, Solomon, Sr.   W-1838   pr 5-p 533, 553
                                                     pr 6-p 155
    4 sons - John, James, David & Solomon Tice   Ludlow Twp.
    Dau - Sarah Newlon

    Exr - John Tice (son)

TILSON, Bethael   E-1824   pr 3-p 257, 412, 437
    (Bethuel)   Union Twp.
    widow - Pamelia
    Heirs - Joseph, Bethuel, Pamela, Richard &
          Cornelia Tilson, minors

    Admr - Augustus Stone

TILTON, Joseph   E-1831   pr 4-p 560, 561
                                                 pr 5-p 165
    widow - Betsey M. Tilton   pr 9-p 223
    6 minor ch - Elizabeth M.,Dudley D., Harriet E.,   Belpre Twp.
              Douglas D., Dallas D.,& Rowena A.
              Tilton (each will get 1/11)

    Admr - John Tilton

*TODD, Nancy Devol   G-1854   pr 9-p 550
    minor dau of Ann F. Todd, late of   B-174
Ohio County, Va. dec'd

    Guardian - James C. Todd of Ohio Co., Va.

TODD, Sally   E-1835   pr 5-p 231
    (dau - of Theophilus Ransom, dec'd)   Marietta,

    Admr - Billy Todd

TOLMAN, Ebenezer   E-1800   pr 1-p 42
    Admr - Seth Tolman   Salem Twp.

TOOMBS, Ira   E-1850   pr 8-p 427, 430
    Admr - Carlton Palmer   Newport Twp.

TOOTHAKER, Horace   E-1830   pr 4-p 451, 452
    Admr - Roger Toothaker   pr 5-p 128
                                                   Fearing Twp.

TREADWELL, John Dexter   W-1835   pr 5-p 174
    (of Salem Twp., Essex Co., Mass.
    where will probated, 1833)

    wife - Dorothy
    son - John Goodline Treadwell
    former domestic - Sarah or Sally Emerson

    Exr - John G. Treadwell (son)

TROWBRIDGE, Herman   E-1824   pr 3-p 162, 281, 282, 465
    (Heman)   pr 4-p 58, 81
    widow - Abigail   Union Twp.
    minor ch - David, Nathaniel, Eliza, Lucinda, Hiram,
          Adaline, Harriet, Theron & Weston (or Watson)

    Admx - Abigail Trowbridge, widow

TRUE, Jabez   W-1823   pr 2-p 441
    Physician   pr 3-p 41, 49, 147
    wife - Sarah   pr 4-p 4
    friend - John Mills   Marietta
    sisters - Hannah True & Mrs. Howard
    nephew - John True Howard, son of said sister Howard
    Julia & Sarah Guitteau, daus of Jonathan Guitteau
         (relation not given)

    Exr - Jno Mills

TRUE, Mrs. Sarah   W-1836   pr 5-p 315, 362, 564
    granddau - Julia Guitteau, wife of John   Marietta
            Hendrick & granddau Sarah Guitteau;
    son - Henry Jackson Mills
    dau - Marietta Mills
    son - John Mills

    Exr - John Mills of Marietta

TUCKER, Mary   E-1824   pr 3-p 167, 406, 436
    heirs - Joshua Tucker, Daniel Tucker, Polly   Marietta
            Tucker (out of state), Betsy Tucker
            (out of state), J. T. Judd & Nancy,
            his wife, with the minor ch of William
            White (James L., Martha & William White, Jr.)

    Admr - John Cotton

TUCKER, Thomas   E-1843   pr 6-p 452, 455
    widow - Eleanor   pr 7-p 383
    no ch under 15 yrs.   Waterford Twp.
    heirs - Samuel, John & Alexander Tucker
            A. J. Higgins, & Robert Reed

    Admrs - William Glines & Alexander Tucker

TUPPER, Benjamin   W-1792   pr 1-p 9, 10
    wife - Huldah   N W Territory
    sons - Anselm, Edward White & minor,   Marietta
            Benjamin, Jr.
    dau - Minerva Nye
    friends - Timothy Meigs (minor son of Return Jonathan
              Meigs); Ebenezer Batelle & Nathaniel Cushing

    Execx - wife, Huldah

TUPPER, Huldah   W-1814   pr 1-p 256
    (widow of Benjamin Tupper)   Marietta

    sons - Anselm Tupper, Edward White Tupper, &
            Benjamin Tupper
    dau - Minerva Nye

    Exrs - Edward White Tupper & Benjamin Tupper

TUTTLE, Augustus C.   E-1839   pr 5-p 591
    widow   pr 6-p 194
    children   Fearing Twp.

    Admx - Martha Tuttle (also called Mary in one place)

```
TUTTLE, David S.               E-1851        pr 8-p 614
    Admr - Joel Tuttle                       pr 9-p 56

TUTTLE, Joel, Sr.              W-1823        pr 2-p 437
    wife - Huldah                            pr 3-p 47, 49, 260
    son - Joel or his heirs                  pr 4-p 40
    other ch - Linus Tuttle; Esther Stephens;   Fearing Twp.
            Simeon Tuttle; Mille Gilbert, Lucy
            Woodruff & Sally West
    adopted son - Preserved Seamen

    Exrs - Simon Porter & Preserved T. Seamen

TUTTLE, Linus                  E-1816        pr 1-p 301
    widow - Mary                             pr 2-p 70, 71
                                             Adams Twp.
    Admr - Amos Porter
    Admx - Mary Tuttle

TUTTLE, Simeon                 E-1817        pr 2-p 45, 460
    widow & heirs mentioned but no names     pr 3-p 549
                                             Fearing Twp.
    Admrs - Joel Tuttle, Jr. & Phebe Tuttle

TWOMBLEY, Hiram                E-1836        pr 5-p 265, 447
    Admr - Joseph Twombley                   Union Twp.

TWOMBLEY, Joseph               W-1842        pr 6-p 311, 361
    wife - Tryphena                          Union Twp.
    10 ch - Josiah, Lydia, Tryphena, Olive, James
            mentioned first; also
    dau - Deborah Chapman Flanders Twombley
    sons - John Hallet Twombley, William Twombley
            & Isaiah Twombley

    Execx - wife, Tryphena Twombley

ULMER, Jacob                   E-1823        pr 2-p 358, 376
    widow - Eleanor                          Marietta
    2 youngest children (not named) are given
            allowance

    Admr - Robert McCabe

VANCLIEF, Mary Ann             W-1852        pr 9-p 226, 290, 291, 296
    children - Daniel Vanclief, Abigail Cheadle,   B-44
            Mary Ann Prisbey, Betsey Morris and
            Leahvina Smith

    Exr - J. C. A. Morris
```

VAN CLIEF, Peter   W-1816   pr 1-p 294
    wife - Mary Ann   pr 2-p 15
    children   Waterford Twp.

    Exrs - wife, Mary Ann & son, Peter

VAN FLEET, Felix W.   E-1839   pr 6-p 25
    Admr - Elias Pewthers, then   pr 7-p 162, 502
    Admr de bonis non - George Gadd   Roxbury Twp.

VAN GILDER, Jeremiah   W-1850   pr 8-p 450, 524
    youngest son - Jesse Hand Vangilder   pr 9-p 112
    2 eldest sons - Hubbard & Amasa Vangilder   Belpre Twp.
    3 daus - Asenath, Clarissa & Louisa M. Vangilder

    Exr - son, Jesse H. Vangilder

VAN LAW, Jeptha   E-1843   pr 6-p 479, 480
    widow - Amy S.   pr 7-p 364
    children   Roxbury Twp.

    Admx - Amy S. Vanlaw

VANWY, Burris   E-1849   pr 8-p 331, 336, 337, 342
(VANWEY, Burrows)   Liberty Twp.
    widow - Esther, insane, has gdn., Elias O. Lennington
            See pr 8-p 338; B-327, 405

    Admr - Elias O. Lennington

VAUGHN, Alexander   E-1853   pr 9-p 448, 449, 527, 583
    widow - Mary M.   B-92, 108, 217
    minor children - Jesse H., John L.   Waterford Twp.

    Admr - S. B. Robinson

VAUGHN, James   E-1842   pr 6-p 352, 353
    Admr - Alexander Vaughn, 2nd   pr 7-p 258
                                                             Waterford Twp.

VAUGHN, Thomas   E-1844   pr 7-p 78, 112, 113
    Admr - Dan C. Lawrence   Waterford Twp.

VIBERT, Anthony   E-1796   pr 1-p 20, 26
    Admr - Francis Joseph Winnocus   Gallipolis, now in
            Devacht   Gallia Co., Ohio

*VINCENT, John   G-1831   pr 4-p 460
    Guardian - Jacob Bridges

                                        Washington County, Ohio Probate -144-

```
*VINCENT, Maria              G-1830              pr 4-p 379
     Guardian - Jacob Bridges

VINCENT, William             E-1825              pr 3-p 401, 534
     widow                                       pr 4-p 117
     family                                      Barlow Twp.

     Admr - Henry E. Vincent

VINCENT, William             W-1846              pr 7-p 304, 344, 453, 454
     2 bros - Thomas & Henry Vincent             pr 8-p 35
     1 sister - Martha Vincent                   Waterford Twp.

     Exr - brother, Henry Vincent

WADSWORTH, Benjamin          W-1826              pr 3-p 504
     (of Danvers, Mass. (Essex Co.)
     where will proved, 1826)

     wife
     grandch - Mary Wadsworth Balch & Elizabeth Balch;
             Betsey Ruggles & John Ruggles;
     dau - Betsey Ruggles, wife of Hon. John Ruggles

     Exr - John Ruggles (son-in-law)

WAIT, Jacob                  E-1850              pr 8-p 430, 440
     Admr - John Collins at Fearing Twp.        Marietta Twp.

WAKEFIELD, Utley             W-1844              pr 7-p 56, 74, 75
     wife - Eleanor                              Newport Twp.
     children - Utley, Jr., Edward, Sally, Liddy,
             Matilda & Lucy Wakefield

     Execx - Eleanor Wakefield

WALKER, David                E-1812              pr 1-p 203
                                                 Salem Twp.

WALKER, Dougall              E-1821              pr 2-p 232, 252
     widow - Mary Walker                         pr 3-p 337
                                                 Wooster Twp. (early
     acting Admr - James Leget in last ref.     name for Watertown Twp.)
     earlier Admr - not named

WARD, Eliza                  W-1847              pr 7-p 463
     (of Providence, R.I. where
     will proved, 1845)

     Exrs - Moses Brown Ives & Joseph Rogers
```

*WARD, Francis Maria   G-1832   pr 4-p 571
    Joseph Buell
    William Hand

    These are children of Mariann B. Ward, dec'd, formerly
    Mariann Buell, dau and heir at law of Joseph Buell, late
    of Marietta, and hence owners of Ohio land which Guardian
    petitions to sell

    Guardian & father - William H. Ward of Rochester,
                   Monroe Co., N.Y.

WARTH, Robert   E-1794   pr 1-p 12
    Admr - bro., John Warth   Marietta

WATERMAN, John   E-1834   pr 5-p 184, 185, 366
    minor ch - under age 15 - Lawrence Waterman   Watertown Twp.
    Admr - John Waterman, Jr.

WATERMAN, Reuben R.   E-1840   pr 6-p 49
    widow & children got year's allowance   pr 7-p 14
    Admr - Theodore Coburn   Waterford Twp.

WATERMAN, Richard   E-1822   pr 2-p 352
    Admr - Jabez True   pr 3-p 288
                                    Marietta

*WATERMAN, Sherman   G-1838   pr 5-p 525
    Guardian - Simeon Deming, Jr.

WATERS, Bernard   W-1839   pr 5-p 534, 582
    mother   Marietta
    younger brother, James Waters
    Exr - Michael Torpy

WATERS, Patrick   W-1852   pr 9-p 113, 190, 196
    minor sons - James L., John B.   B-26
    Execx - wife, Mary S. Waters   Marietta

WATSON, John   W-1851   pr 8-p 589
    (of East Windsor, Hartford Co.,
    Conn. where will proved 1824)

    wife
    oldest son - John Watson, Jr.
    daus - Polly (Mary) Pudor & Nancy Hall
    granddau - Sarah Ann Perry
    children of son, Henry & ch of son, William

    Exrs - sons, William & Henry Watson

WEAVER, George G.   E-1853   pr 9-p 483
      widow - Susan   B-102, 144
      Admr - Thomas Ewart   Marietta

*WEBSTER, John   G-1852   pr 9-p 104
      Mary
      Andrew
      Lucy

      children of John L. Webster, dec'd
      widow, Mary Webster, also mentioned

      Guardian - William McNeal

WEBSTER, Samuel Hollen   E-1816   pr 1-p 310
      (of Danvers, Mass., (Essex Co.)

      Admr - George Osgood, Jr., physician of Danvers, Mass.

WEIDNER, Joseph   E-1849   pr 8-p 362, 379
      no wife mentioned   pr 9-p 123
      minor ch - given year's support (See gdn's B-6
      Acct. for Stephen & Frederick - pr 9- p 118 -   Fearing Twp.
      gdn - Gerlock Kremer)

      Admr - Michael Weidner

*WEIDNER, Stephen   G-1852   pr 9-p 118
      Frederick   B-6

      minor sons of Joseph Weidner, deceased

      Guardian - Gerlock Kremer

WEIGEL, Jeremiah, Jr.   E-1853   pr 9-p 346, 397
      4 minor children   B-62
      Admx - Dorothy Weigel (widow)   Union Twp.

WELLS, Joseph   E-1825   pr 3-p 366, 395
      widow   Adams Twp.

      Admr - Joseph C. Wells

*WELLS, Julia A.   G-1853   pr 9-p 490
      minor dau of Robert Wells, dec'd   B-140, 141

      Guardian - brother, William C. Wells

WELLS, Robert   W-1852   pr 9-p 252, 424, 464, 490
      wife - Hannah   B-53
      daus - Mary, Susanna, Elizabeth, Rebecca, Harriet Wells Marietta Twp.
      sons - Timothy & William Case Wells
      also daus - Polly Hannah & Julia Adelia Wells

      Exrs - wife, Hannah & son, Timothy Wells

WELLS, Thomas   E-1790   pr 1-p 4, 5
      eldest son - Clark Wells   Marietta

      Admrs - sons - Joseph Wells & David Wells

WESTGATE, George   E-1810   pr 1-p 187, 197
      Admr - Calvin Rechold (Reckard)   Marietta

WESTON, Samuel   W-1840   pr 6-p 86
      wife - Eliza Ann   Marietta Twp.
      parents' estate in Huntington Co., Pa.

      Exr - Joseph L. Record (father-in-law)

WHEELER, Otis   E-1850   pr 8-p 389, 391, 506, 507
      widow & child   pr 9-p 441
            B-300
      Admr - William Slocomb   Marietta

WHIPPLE, Abraham   W-1819   pr 2-p 139
      wife - Sarah   Fearing Twp.
      dau - Katherine Sproat, widow of late Col.
            Ebenezer Sproat
      grandson - Ebenezer Sproat Sibley
      grandson - Henry Hastings Sibley

      Joint Exrs - wife, Sarah & dau, Katherine Sproat

WHIPPLE, Levi   W-1845   pr 7-p 179, 294
      wife - Eliza   pr 8-p 194
      sons - Warren W., Edward Augustus, Francis   pr 9-p 197
            R., & William Wells Whipple   (of Harmar now, but late
      daus - Eliza W. Putnam & Lucy R. Allen   of Muskingum Co., Ohio)
      niece - Lucy Maria Whipple &
      nephew - Rev. George Warner

      Exrs - Eliza Whipple & son-in-law, Douglas Putnam

WHITE, David   E-1841   pr 6-p 173, 396
      Admrs - Charles S. Cory & Asa White   Waterford Twp.

WHITE, Harris   E-1842   pr 6-p 422, 431
      widow & 4 ch got year's allowance but   pr 7-p 343
            are unnamed   pr 8-p 284, 286
            Waterford Twp.
      Admr - Seneca Clark & Admx - Frances White
      then, Admr de bonis non - Augustin S. Clark

WHITE, James   E-1852   pr 9-p 200
      widow - Deborah   B-9
      5 minor ch under age of 15   Marietta Twp.

      Admr - William White

WHITE, John H.   W-1827   pr 4-p 63, 113, 273
    wife - Matilda   Fearing Twp.
    ch - George L. White, Mary Ann White, James Howell White,
        Edward T. White, Abraham Whipple White, Esther Leavens
        White, & Hannah Matilda White; also, second son, Isaac
        Williams White

    Execx - Matilda White (wife)

WHITNEY, Elisha   W-1839   pr 5-p 568
    (of Beverly, Mass., Essex Co.,
    where will probated, 1807)

    wife - Eunice
    children

    Execx - wife, Eunice Whitney

WHITNEY, John   W-1849   pr 8-p 345
    wife   Waterford Twp.
    children, under age - no names

    Exr - wife but no name given

WHITNEY, William   E-1849   pr 8-p 327, 330
    Admr - Davis Green   pr 9-p 195, 317

WHITTOCK, Maria   W-1850   pr 8-p 517
    Sister, Sophia Collins, wife of John Collins   Fearing Twp.
            of Fearing Twp. formerly Sophia Whittock

    Exr - John Collins

WHITTOCK, William   W-1822   pr 2-p 269, 369
    son - Henry   Fearing Twp.
    dau - Elizabeth
    other ch - John, William, Samuel, Sophia,
            and Maria Whittock

    Exr - Sam Whittock

WIGHT, Ephraim C.   E-1824   pr 3-p 130, 133
    Admx - Rhoda Wight   pr 4-p 28
                                                Waterford Twp.

WILBER, Constant   E-1795   pr 1-p 18
    Admr - John Peter Romain Bureau of   Gallipolis Twp., later
        Gallipolis   in Gallia Co.

WILCOX, Joseph M.   E-1818   pr 2-p 62
    Admr - Caleb Emerson

WILKES, Charles   W-1835   pr 5-p 176
  (of New York City, where
  will probated, 1833)

   wife - Janet
   3 sons - Horatio, George & Hamilton Wilkes
   daus - Charlotte Jeffrey, Fanny Golden & Ann Wilkes
   also - niece, nephews and friend

   Exrs - wife, Janet & 3 sons, above listed

WILLARD, Rev. Joseph   E-1823   pr 3-p 25, 267, 537
   Children - George I. Willard; Caroline Willcox, pr 4-p 52, 73
      wife of Henry P. Willcox; Elizabeth Marietta
      Carpenter, wife of Thomas Carpenter
      of New York City; Joseph Willard (minor)
      of Pike Co., Ohio; Ellen Willard of New
      York City; & Peter Willard of Parkersburg, Va.

   Admr - George I. Willard, followed by
   Admr de bonis non -William Slocomb

WILLIAMS, Thomas W.   E-1851   pr 9-p 80, 96
   Admr - Artemas W. Williams   Marietta
   Admx - Mary M. Williams (widow)

WILLIAMS, William   W-1804/5   pr 1-p 66, 67
                  Waterford Twp.

   wife - Martha
   sons - William & Ahira

   Exr - Simeon Deming

WILLIAMSON, Moses   W-1806   pr 1-p 78, 125
   wife - Christiana   Grandview Twp.
   legatee - Jacob Brown, son of Andrew &
       Susannah Brown
   brothers & sisters - not named but David Williamson,
       son of Jeremiah Williamson, dec'd is to
       get his father's share

   Exrs - wife, Christiana & bro. Samuel Williamson

WILLIAMSON, Robert   W-1850   pr 8-p 452
   Exr - William Pitt Racer   Marietta

WILLIAMSON, Samuel   W-1808   pr 1-p 123, 168, 178
   wife - Deborah   Grandview Twp.
   sons - Moses, James, William & Samuel
   daus - Ruth Williamson, Jane Caldwell, Mary Mills,
     Elizabeth Bayson & Sarah Williamson

   Exrs - wife, Deborah & son, Samuel Williamson

WILMARTH, Rufus W.   E-1838   pr 5-p 514
    Heirs - R. P. Orm, A. J. Wilmarth & admr. James   pr 6-p 87
        Ormiston for wife Lucinda's share   pr 8-p 154
    Admr - James Ormiston   Wesley Twp.

WILLSON, William   E-1797   pr 1-p 28
    Admr - George Willson   Waterford Twp.

WILSON, Amos   W-1837   pr 5-p 384, 429, 433, 434
    wife - Elizabeth   pr 6-p 199
    sons - Newell, Nelson & Charles   Adams Twp.
    daus - Eliza Williams; Polly Lewis
    grandch - Caroline & Emeline Lake;
              Lorenzo Wilson

    Exr - Otis O. Lewis (son-in-law)

WILSON, Elizabeth   E-1849   pr 8-p 363, 365, 382
    minor ch - Martha Jane Knowlton; William   pr 9-p 61
               Knowlton, Robert N. Wilson
               & George Wilson

    Admr - Richard Scott at Ludlow Twp.

WILSON, Elwood   E-1853   pr 9-p 497
    of Noble Co., Ohio   B-96, 110

    widow - Jane
    minor ch - Rhoda Elizabeth, Eleanor Eliza, Nancy
               Delilah and William Alonzo Wilson

    Admr - John C. Paxton

WILSON, George   E-1808   pr 1-p 113, 313
    Admr - Jesse Davis   Waterford Twp.

WILSON, Isaac   E-1851   pr 8-p 584, 586
    widow - dau - son   pr 9-p 54, 397
    Admr - Alexander McGirr   Decatur Twp.

WILSON, Jonathan   E-1841   pr 6-p 203
    widow - Mary   Roxbury Twp.
    Admr - Hiram Gard

WILSON, Sarah   W-1838   pr 5-p 480
    (widow of Rev. Andrew Wilson of   Marietta
    Washington, Pa., but now of Marietta, Ohio)
    son - James D. Wilson
    son -   Wilson of Washington, Pa.

    Exr - John Cotton of Marietta

WILSON, Thomas   E-1823   pr 3-p 61, 62, 458
     widow   pr 4-p 2
     children - Lydia Waterman, wife of Horace   Wooster Twp. (early name
           Waterman; Betsy Bosworth, wife of   for Watertown Twp.)
           Charles Bosworth; Nancy Waterman,
           wife of Sherman Waterman, admr.
     minors - Nathaniel, Roger, John, Mary & Ephraim Wilson;
           also, William Wilson, resident of Maine

     Admr - Sherman Waterman

WILSON, William   E-1849   pr 8-p 265, 273, 315, 552
     widow   Ludlow Twp.
     children under age 15

     Admr - Alexander Bell

WILSON, William   E-1849   pr 8-p 339, 340, 343
     widow - Covina Wilson   pr 9-p 11
     heirs - Elijah & Stephen Wilson   Watertown Twp.

     Admr - Isaac Johnson

WINCHELL, John G.   E-1851   pr 8-p 579, 580
(WEINCHAEL)

     widow - Mary Barber Winchell
     minor ch - J. Pall Winchell

     Admr - George Weigel

WINN, Timothy   W-1828   pr 4-p 178
     (of Salem, Mass., Essex County, where
     will probated, 1827)

     Sister - Nancy Richardson of Woburn, Mass.
     Brother - Thales Winn of Salem, Mass.
     ½ Sister - Caroline Winn of Woburn, Mass
     children of late bro, Samuel Winn - Emily Elliot
           of Beverly and Sarah Winn

     Exrs - Uncles - Joseph Winn & John Winn & cousin, John Winn, Jr.

WINSOR, Henry   E-1828   pr 4-p 234, 236, 395, 501
     widow - Anna   Waterford Twp.
     minor children - Betsey & Augustus

     Admr - Joseph Arnold

WISEMAN, Sarah   W-1823   pr 2-p 421
               (non-cupative will)   pr 3-p 124, 125
     heirs - Nancy Mixer, wife of Isaac Mixer;   Marietta
           children of David Gilmore, dec'd,
           John, Sarah, Isaac & David; - Sarah,wife of Jude Hamilton

     Exr - William Skinner

WITHINGTON, William   E-1808   pr 1-p 125, 173, 270
    Admr - Isaac Peirce   Belpre Twp.

WITHROW, James   E-1849   pr 8-p 269, 294, 309
    widow   Marietta
    2 minor children - William Wallace and James -
                see gdn. accts - pr 9-p 439
    Admr - Joseph E. Hall

*WITHROW, William Wallace   G-1853   pr 9-p 439, 440
        James N.   B-329
    minor heirs of James Withrow
    Guardian - James Dunn

WITZ, Daniel   W-1846   pr 7-p 381
    Written in German Script   Salem Twp.

WOOD, Joseph   W-1852   pr 9-p 99, 119, 171
    Sons - Paulus Emelius Wood; Caius Martius Wood B-5
    grandsons - oldest 2 sons of Paulus Emelius Wood Marietta
    grandson - Joseph, son of Caius Martius Wood
    dau - Agness Wood
    Exr - Caius Martius Wood

WOODBRIDGE, Dudley   E-1824   pr 3-p 158, 161, 232
    heirs - John, Dudley, Jr. & William Woodbridge; pr 4-p 278, 398, 457
        William W. Petit, Sally Matthews, Dudley   Marietta
        Woodbridge Petit, Alexander Hamilton Matthews
        & minor, David Woodbridge Matthews
    Admr - James M. Booth

WOODBRIDGE, Dudley   W-1853   pr 9-p 382, 425, 464
    wife - Maria (Mrs. M. M.)   B-78
    daus - Jane G. Morgan, Lucy Smith, Maria M.   Marietta
        Woodbridge
    sons - George M., John M., William & David
    Exrs - wife - Maria, friend - Anselm T. Nye and
        sons - George M. & John M. Woodbridge

WOODS, Stephen   W-1791   pr 1-p 6, 9
    (1st U.S. Regt.,   (non-cupative will)
    Capt. Heart's Company)
    legatee - Solomon Phelps, soldier in same company
    Admr - Paul Fearing

WOODWARD, Elihu   E-1823   pr 2-p 343
    widow - Ruth   pr 3-p 115, 187
    family mentioned - no names   pr 4-p 79
    land held in common witn Oliver Woodward, Jr., Marietta
    who was gdn. of his heirs

    Admx - Ruth Woodward, widow

WRIGHT, Jotham   E-1823   pr 2-p 343
    Admx - Eleanor Wright   pr 3-p 187
                                               Newport Twp.

WURSTER, Frederic   E-1852   pr 9-p 327, 328, 329
    widow - Barbery Wurster   B-49, 61
    minor ch - Jacob, Adam, Maria   Aurelius Twp.

    Admr - John Snider

WYLLYS, Samuel   W-1836   pr 5-p 333
  (of Hartford, Conn.
  where will proved, 1823)

    dau - Mary W. Gannett, wife of John M. Gannett, Esq.
    son - Oliver St.John Wyllys
    son - William Alfred Wyllys

    Exr - William Talcott

YALE, Aaron   W-1820   pr 2-p 203, 275, 277
    son - Stephen   Adams Twp.
    grand ch - William & Sarah Taylor
    son - Aaron
    daus - Phally Curtis, Anne Gentle, Polly Barton
        & Salley Alley

    Exr - Jesse Baldwin

YEO, Charles   E-1852   pr 9-p 348, 349, 476
    widow - Mary Yeo   B-45, 103, 105, 107
    minor ch - Charles; of full age - Elizabeth Ann Yeo Marietta

    Admr - John Collins

YORK, James   E-1790   pr 1-p 5
    soldier in service of the U. S.

    Admr - Capt David Zeigler

YOUNG, Henry   E-1804   pr 1-p 59, 60
                                                 Marietta

www.ingramcontent.com/pod-product-compliance
Lightning Source LLC
Chambersburg PA
CBHW050527270326
41926CB00015B/3107